The Murray Family

History and Heritage from Lena's Trunk

Helen Murray White

HERITAGE BOOKS
2019

HERITAGE BOOKS
AN IMPRINT OF HERITAGE BOOKS, INC.

Books, CDs, and more—Worldwide

For our listing of thousands of titles see our website
at
www.HeritageBooks.com

Published 2019 by
HERITAGE BOOKS, INC.
Publishing Division
5810 Ruatan Street
Berwyn Heights, Md. 20740

Heritage Books by the author:

Butterfield Overland Mail Route: History of Early Settlers
Along Boonville Rd in Northern Greene County [Missouri]

The Murray Family: History and Heritage from Lena's Trunk

Layout and design by Lean McKay

International Standard Book Number
Paperbound: 978-0-7884-5806-4

Dedication

This book is dedicated to all the strong women.

Contents

Acknowledgements

I could not have written this story without the documents which I found in the family trunk. I am indebted to the grandmothers who kept everything in good condition, so that one day I could research and tell the family story.

Grandmother Lena placed them in the trunk which she inherited from her mother. I doubt that Lena realized the significance of the documents; she saved them because she never threw anything away.

What is remarkable is that the papers were not lost in the move from Ohio to Missouri, or that after Huldah's death, someone did not clean the house and throw loose papers in the fire. The young children could have cut, marked on, or destroyed the papers. Thankfully, they didn't.

After Lena re-married, my father and mother lived in Huldah's house. I don't think either of them investigated what was in the trunk. They simply added their own items for safekeeping. My father didn't care about what was in the trunk, or in answering my questions about what I had found. Perhaps the documents survived because no one was very interested in them.

Thanks to Nicholas Pavlik and his staff at Bowling Green State University, Bowling Green, Ohio, for their research in early Wyandot County records. Their assistance answered many questions about Mary Murray.

I couldn't have put this work together without the enthusiasm and creativity of Lean McKay.

Anne Baker at Special Collections and Archives, Missouri State University, Springfield, Missouri, was very helpful in organizing materials and accepting the papers for permanent preservation.

Thanks to my family members, in particular my husband, for continued support and encouragement.

Helen Murray White

Introduction

Opening The Trunk

I discovered the family trunk in the attic when I was very young. It was filled with all kinds of interesting items: old clothing, pictures, a box of memorabilia from World War I, books, and flour sacks filled with letters, receipts, and legal documents.

The name on the trunk, "Wilhelmina Muller," meant that it belonged to my great-grandmother. The date, 1869, indicated that it must have been given to her for her dowry. When Wilhelmina, her husband, and two little girls, immigrated to America in 1873, it was large enough to carry the family's household possessions. Because it was rounded on top, it was the preferred type of trunk for ship travel. No other trunk could be placed on top of it.

Somehow my grandmother Lena inherited the trunk. One sister left the county and never returned, the other sister died, and the two brothers probably were not interested in the old thing. Being true to her German heritage, Lena never threw anything away, keeping letters, pieces of string and packets of buttons and thread. She kept documents which predated her presence in the family.

The first items that caught my eye were letters from someone named Z.G. Murray. But they were from a man who lived in Ohio. My grandfather, Z.G., lived in Missouri. Who was this man from Ohio? To answer that question, I started looking for relatives in Ohio and that led the search to New York.

I treasured the documents I found, not really knowing the significance of most of them. Going to the trunk, opening it, and finding a new tidbit made me feel like a child opening Christmas presents. There was always a surprise. I looked at the papers in the trunk and lovingly put them away, knowing that one day in a few weeks, or months, or years, I would open the trunk and find them again. I never really wanted to get to the bottom of the trunk.

Reluctantly, about seventy years later, I reached the bottom of the trunk, took out all the flour sacks and began sorting the papers, deciding which ones had historical significance and which ones had to be thrown away. Those were difficult decisions.

I had lived with these documents for years, trying to make sense of them and following genealogy trails that led to surprising new facts—or to nothing at all. After years of searching, I knew the family story, but how would someone else make sense of the papers and documents without knowing the story? Because descendants had long ago left their original homes and some family lines had disappeared, it seemed crucial to write what I had learned before the history and memories were lost forever. It would be so easy for someone to throw all the papers and documents into a nearby dumpster.

I also learned that family stories are not totally accurate. They often contain just a kernel of truth, providing a clue for further investigation. That's why genealogy is so compelling—it is a continuing mystery, one that may never be solved.

This is the story of the Murray families in Missouri, Ohio and New York, describing what their lives were like from the time George Murray fought as a soldier in the French and Indian War, until his descendants settled in Missouri. George had many descendants, some of whom may want to learn about the family; perhaps this book will help in their research.

The Murray Family is an ordinary family with no famous people or connections to royalty. Some achieved success in their vocations, many were community leaders, and yet, there were some with questionable reputations. Their stories, however, describe lives interwoven with historic events that shaped our country.

Original documents were donated to the Missouri State University Library at Missouri State University, Springfield, Missouri. They are available for research only. Contact: Special Collections and Archives at 417.836.5428 or Archives@missouristate.edu.

1

George Murray
in the French and Indian War

The progenitor of this Murray family in the United States was George Murray, said to have been born 12 September, 1731, in Inverness, Scotland; who died prior to the probate of his will on 28 August, 1793, in Orange County, New York.

There have been two stories about his origin. First, the glorified version found in Rutenber's, *History of Orange County, New York*. The author stated that George Murray was with Wolfe in the battle for Quebec during the French and Indian War, and "acquitted himself nobly." (1) Since family historians have stated that George was born in Inverness, at first glance one might believe that he was a member of Fraser's Highlanders. The Highlanders enlisted at Inverness and served under General Wolfe. They assembled in Inverness, embarked at Glasgow in 1757, and spent the winter of 1757-58 in Connecticut. They were the only Highland troops present at the Battle of the Plains of Abraham in Canada. Between 1760 and 1763, they were garrisoned in Montreal, Quebec and Nova Scotia.

Stories on the internet relate interesting tales about the Highlanders, their bravery and ability to withstand freezing temperatures dressed in their kilts. A General Murray, who was Scottish, fought with General James Wolfe, at the battle for Quebec; but he was not our ancestor.

Spencer Murray, a descendant of William Murray, who was one of George Murray's sons, believes that George Murray was connected to the Duke of Atholl, head of the Murray clan in Inverness. This is a great story, and although it cannot be proven, provides Murray descendants with a link to Scottish history.

The Murrays take their name from the province of Moray, brought under the Scottish realm in the twelfth century. Flemish war lords across the North Sea aided the Scottish kings in bringing law and order to the Welsh border. They subsequently intermarried with royals from the house of Moray and their descendants assumed the surname of Moray or Murray. By the seventeenth century, the Murrays had acquired over 200,000 acres in the Scottish Highlands. Since 1703, the Murray chiefs have been called Dukes of Atholl, adopting as their family motto, "Furth Fortune and Fill the Fetters." Their tartan is composed of dark green and dark blue plaids with a bright red accent line. The Blair Castle, at Blair Atholl, is still the home of the current Duke of Atholl, and is claimed as the home of the descendants of the name Murray.

However there is no research to prove our Murray connection with nobility. Our George Murray was more likely to have been a serf working on the manor.

There is a more probable story about George Murray obtained from a posting on Ancestry.com quoting from Ada Murray Safford. Unfortunately Ms. Murray Safford's papers are designated as "private" and are unavailable to the public. According to her post: "George enlisted in Inverness, Scotland. He came to Virginia as a soldier in the British Army under Braddock, the 44th Regiment, in the campaign of 1755. He was in Col. Dunbar's Company at Braddock's defeat at Fort Duquesne. The fort was at the junction of the Allegheny and Monongahela Rivers, which is now downtown Pittsburg. George lost a leg there, was picked up by a Dutch farmer, and nursed back to health by the man's daughter, Mary Jane Snyder, whom George married."

This is a good story, but there are some facts which bear investigating.

There are many accounts about the Braddock expedition in 1755. The expedition was a debacle from the beginning. There are those who said that Braddock was a mediocre general; others praised his ability. His real problem was that he had no experience fighting Indians and was reluctant to follow the advice of the American settlers who had years of experience. He said that one British soldier was equal to four French or Indians. Sadly, his arrogance was his downfall.

In order to get the troops to Fort Duquesne, the army had to slog through the mountains of western Pennsylvania, cutting their way through forests and swamps, and following trails made by early traders. The procession of troops, slaves, wives, camp followers, guns, and supplies stretched for miles. Some of the cannons and heavy artillery had to be left behind as the army made its way through narrow gorges. One of those gorges is where the nine hundred French and Indians attacked. General Braddock knew only how to fight as he had been trained from the British manuals, and in addition, the soldiers' red coats and silver swords made them easy targets.

The Indians attacked, shooting from behind trees and rocks, virtually invisible to the British soldiers. The British returned fire, shooting in all directions, and seeing no targets, accidentally shot their own men. Braddock heroically tried to rally his troops before he sustained a wound from which he died four days later. At the end of the battle, 500 British soldiers were dead, nearly 500 were wounded, and only 300 escaped unharmed. Those who could escape found their way back to Dunbar's company (about twenty miles away) and avoided being scalped, imprisoned or tortured by the Indians.

Perhaps George Murray escaped to Dunbar's company or perhaps he had been wounded earlier as Braddock's and Dunbar's regiments began their impossible trek. After Braddock died, Dunbar retreated to Philadelphia. This part of the story would correspond with the family history that George Murray lost his leg and a Dutch farmer and family helped him recuperate. He could not continue with the Army because he would no longer be of any value to the Army.

There is an interesting puzzle here however. The 44th Regiment (Braddock's) and the 48th Regiment (Dunbar's) were composed of Irish soldiers. They were the two Irish regiments that fought in the French and Indian War. McCardell, in his biography of Braddock said, "The Forty-Fourth and the Forty-Eighth were two of the most worthless regiments in the army. And the drafts with which their depleted ranks were filled brought together all the least desirable soldiers of the six other regiments from which they were drawn. Such drafts always produced the dregs. The colonels had no intention of losing their best men." (2)

This poses the question: Was George Murray Irish or Scottish? The question may never be answered. There were numerous Murray families who lived in

England, Scotland and Ireland. Since the British Army only listed officers by name, it is doubtful that there was a record listing George Murray as either a volunteer or an impressed soldier.

A direct descendant recently received a DNA report from Twenty-three and Me, a DNA research site. The report showed Irish and English ancestry, but no Scottish ancestry.

There is another factor to consider. After the swell of Irish immigrants in the middle nineteenth century, the Irish became the lowest rung of American society. When telling the family history, was it better to claim Scottish ancestry, rather than Irish?

Bibliography
(1) Ruttenber, E.M. and Clark, L.H. *History of Orange County, New York.* Philadelphia: Everts & Peck, 1881.

(2) McCardell, Lee. *Ill-Stared General: Braddock of the Coldstream Guards.* University of Pittsburg Press, 1958.

2

George Murray in Orange County, New York

Much of the information written about George Murray comes from family stories, undocumented and unproven. It has been a challenge to locate facts. Some of the information has to be paired with historical events, leaving the researcher to imagine what *might* have happened.

The story of George Murray during the French and Indian War has been told in the previous chapter, but what was happening to the settlers who lived in Pennsylvania, New Jersey and New York during that time period?

Settlers in those states were constantly harassed by the Indians. When E.M. Ruttenber gave his address to the Newburgh New York Historical Society in 1885, he described the terrible border conditions. "The settlements west of the Wallkill were perpetually harassed, and many of them broken up; men were killed in the fields and in their houses; women and children became the victims of the scalping knife."

The French and Indian War began as a territorial war. For years the settlers had been encroaching on lands of the local Indian tribes. The treaty of Aix la Chapelle in 1748 had defined boundaries between the French and the English. The agreement was that the "subjects of France, inhabitants of Canada, were not to disturb or molest the Five Indian Nations who were the subjects of Great Britain." This agreement was ignored as the French set about building forts all along the Mississippi River to New Orleans and Virginia sent out the Ohio Company in order to populate the Ohio River Valley. The Indians complained that the whites appropriated lands belonging to them.

When tribal leaders expressed their grievances to British authorities, they were ignored; consequently, the tribes banded together and become allies with the

French. According to Clearwater in his book, *The History of Ulster County, New York*, "The Delaware Indians had been defrauded of their land… by the purchasers of the Minisink lands who had made them drunk and refused to pay them when sober." (1) Ruttenber detailed some of the horrendous retaliatory acts committed by the Indians on the border settlers. (2)

Colonel Thomas Ellison wrote the General Assembly of New York in 1757, regarding the conditions of the early settlers. "It is but too well known by the late numerous murders barbarously committed on our borders, that the county of Ulster and the north end of Orange is become the only frontier part of the province left unguarded and exposed to the cruel incursions of the Indian enemy, and the inhabitants of these parts have been obliged to perform very hard military duty for these two years past, in ranging the woods and guarding the frontiers…." Colonel Ellison later added that the inhabitants were exhausted. (2)

There are no family stories about how long George and Mary resided in Pennsylvania or when they came to Orange County (Ulster County at that time). Did they experience some of the horrors of living in the Pennsylvania wilderness? Did they move east to seek protection with other settlers in forts located in Ulster and Orange counties? When did they purchase their land and how did they acquire money for that purchase?

Research in early land records of Ulster and Orange counties did not show any land transactions for George Murray in the years between 1756 and 1793. It is probable that any land he purchased was not recorded because there was no legal requirement to record a deed at that time.

Because settlers were limited to patents of no more than 2,000 acres, and individuals could join together in patent purchases, settlements in Orange and Ulster counties consisted of small, family-sized farms. It is believed that George became a farmer, which was a definite possibility, since most of these settlers made their living by farming. "The colonies of New York, New Jersey and Pennsylvania—and particularly the Hudson Valley—were known as the breadbasket of the British Empire." (3) The basic crop of Orange County was wheat, followed in later years by dairying.

George and Mary's possessions may have resembled those of Sarah Wells, the first white settler in Goshen in 1714. Sarah brought two horses with bells on, two milk cows with bells, two Irish Brahmas, one spade, two pails, two beds and bedding, one small and one large kettle, wood trenchers and bowls, candlesticks and candles, coffeepot with coffee, teapot, chocolate, tin canister with tea, a pair of trammels, a frying pan, small tin plates with saucers, a bundle of cloths, saddlebags, pillow saddles, knives and forks, some potatoes, wallets, medical cordials in vials, refined sugar in small pieces, brown sugar in rolls, flour, biscuits, ham in small sacks and some trinkets, ribbons and small knives for Indians. Judged by the standards of the day, Sarah appeared to be fairly well-off. Did George and Mary have as many possessions as Sarah when they came to Ulster County? I think it is doubtful.

The couple had eight sons and one daughter. Alexander was the only son born in Pennsylvania. There is no reliable record of their marriage date. A posting on Ancestry.com indicated that they were married in 1756, but the time span between marriage date and birth of their first son seems highly unusual.

Later records indicated that Alexander's birthday was sometime around 1765. If this is true, the date would indicate that George and Mary moved to Ulster County, New York after 1765 and before 1767. George would have settled in Ulster County before the American Revolution began.

Orange County played a significant role during the Revolutionary War because the Hudson River Valley became a major battle objective of the British forces. In addition to the British desire to split the New England colonies from the Middle and Southern colonies, the Hudson River was crucial for transportation. The best location for preventing the British movement up the Hudson was at Fort Defiance (later known as West Point), where the river changes course at an acute angle. A sailing ship would be moving at a slow speed either above or below the point, depending upon the wind direction. Whichever side controlled that point could limit access or permit access northward to Albany. The British had an almost successful seizure of the point in 1777.

The western boundary of Orange County was the Delaware River. In 1779, while the British forces were fighting on Manhattan Island, Joseph Brant, a Mohawk chief who had been given the rank of Captain in the British Army, was sent to gather intelligence around Minisink, Orange County. In July, he found that most of the Delaware Valley was undefended.

With that information, Brant put together a force of sixty tribesmen and twenty-seven Tories disguised as Indians, and forced settlers to flee their homes. A militia was formed in Goshen, Orange County, to oppose Brant's forces, led by Lt. Colonel Benjamin Tusten. He opposed engaging Brant's army because he knew the settlers would be no match for the army, but the public and militia demanded retribution. The militia, led by Tusten, met Brant's forces at the Minisink Ford and was defeated after being surrounded and outnumbered. Forty-eight militia men were killed, as well as Lt. Colonel Tusten.

By 1781, the Americans determined that a large military force was necessary in the Hudson Valley to keep the British occupied while battles were occurring in New York City. George Washington set up headquarters in Newburgh, Orange County. He stayed in the Jonathan Hasbrouck house for seventeen months, directing the operation against Lord Cornwallis, who subsequently surrendered to Washington.

This description identified Orange and Ulster counties as crucial in the battle for American independence. Many citizens from these counties later participated in the Continental Congress and organization of the new country. George and Mary were living in Ulster County by this time.

George Murray's sons would have been too young to serve in the Revolutionary War, although his sons, George and Jacob served in the War of 1812. It is possible that George was a supporter of the rebellion; a George Murray was listed in the Ulster County Militia, Second Regiment, as a recipient of Land Bounty Rights. I believe that this is the George of this family line, because the boundary line between Orange County and Ulster County was not settled by statute until 1801, and George's will was filed in Ulster County.

In 1774, the New York legislature noted that the "line dividing the Counties of Ulster and Orange, has never been run and marked further west than the east side of the Shawangunk Mountains...." It ordered a new survey. In 1798, five townships of Ulster County were moved into Orange County: New Windsor, Newburgh, Wallkill, Montgomery and Deerpark. The New York Legislature fixed the new border by statute on 3 April, 1801. With such a confusing past, it is no surprise that land records are spotty.

The topic of land bounty rights was found in *New York in the Revolution as Colony and State Volume I*, which described that early land rights (500 acres) were offered to officers and men for two regiments raised for defense of the state. As the war progressed and more men were needed, the government upped the ante. By March, 1782, an act was passed which provided that any class or any person who furnished an able-bodied man to serve for three years during the war, should be entitled to 600 acres; or 350 acres for a two years' enlistment; and any person or class who should deliver a man within twenty days from the time of notification, 200 acres extra. (4)

George would have been in his fifties when he was listed in the Ulster County Militia—almost too old to serve. Men sixty and older were classified as "exempts." These were the men who were "exempt from field service by reason of age or infirmities, previous service, professional occupation, etc., but who, nevertheless, during the Revolution, were regularly enrolled, made liable to service, in emergencies, and subject to a special tax for the purchase of arms and to supply men in the active force." Clearwater said, "To the honors of service in the Revolution they are as fully entitled as were the men who were on the active roll." (1) As an example, Quakers, Moravians and United Brethren were enrolled, but exempt from service on payment of money. By 1780, they were obliged to pay 160 pounds per year.

George would not have been fit to serve since he had lost a leg in the French and Indian War, but by the terms of enrollment, he was required to contribute toward furnishing and equipping another man. Then the question arises, "Did he add to the land he owned by providing men for the regiments?"

The land inherited and sold by his three youngest sons was described as being bounded on the south by the line that formerly divided the counties of Orange and Ulster. This description would further verify that George owned property in Ulster County. The boundary lines of Orange County, as set by the legislature in 1801 were: "all that part of this State bounded southerly by the state of New Jersey, westerly by the State of Pennsylvania, easterly by the middle of the Hudson River, and northerly by an east and west line from the mouth of Murderer's Creek." Murderer's Creek, also known as Moodna Creek, is located south of the town of Newburgh and empties into the Hudson River.

George Murray wrote his will 21 September, 1792, and it was probated 28 August, 1793, in Ulster County. He gave five shillings each to his five eldest sons, Alexander, James, John, George and William and all of his land to his three youngest sons, David, Jacob and Charles. He noted that when David became age twenty-one, the shares should be equally divided between them, and until the younger ones become of age (Jacob and Charles), the land should be put to use for them. He gave his daughter Mary, ten pounds lawful money and to Mary, the daughter of George, he gave five pounds of lawful money of New York. After all expenses were paid, he asked for the balance to be divided between "my wife Mary, my three sons David, Jacob and Charles, daughter Mary and my two granddaughters Eleanor, the daughter of John, and Mary, the daughter of George, heretofore mentioned." He also asked that the sum of five pounds be given to the poor of "that society to which my wife belongs." A line following the names of witnesses, David Wandle, Saml Tooker and Abel Woodhull, stated "John's daughter excluded from anything and so are the–(unintelligible)." The court appointed James Murray as executor of the estate.

His will enumerated George's children probably stated in the order of their births. The older sons, given only five shillings each, were established in the community and he may have felt that they did not need an inheritance. There had been land purchases by the older sons before George's death. Evidently they had money.

By giving land to his three minor sons, he gave them the opportunity to become land owners. It is surprising that he had only fifty-six acres for their inheritance. If he acquired land by military bounty rights, perhaps he had already given that land to the oldest sons. He names two granddaughters in his will, raising the questions: "Were these his only grandchildren at the time of his death? Why did he exclude the daughter of John, without giving her name? Was she the same daughter, Eleanor, named earlier to inherit a part of his estate?" The five pounds given to his wife's charity indicates that she was committed to religious or social causes. There are no records of Mary Snyder Murray's death or how long she lived after George's will was filed.

Bibliography

(1) Clearwater, Alphonso T. *The History of Ulster County, New York.* Kingston, New York: W.J. Van Deusen, 1907.

(2) Ruttenber and Clark. *History of Orange County, New York.* Philadelphia: Everts & Peck, 1881.

(3) Booth, Malcolm, "A Short History of Orange County N.Y." Sponsored by The Orange County Chamber of Commerce.

(4) *New York in the Revolution as Colony and State, Volume I.* Albany, New York: J.B. Lyon Company, 1904.

George Murray's will.

3

Children of
George and Mary Jane Murray

There are many published records about the children of George and Mary Murray which provide glimpses into their everyday activities and illustrate how their lives were interwoven with historic events in the United States.

George and Mary Jane had eight sons and one daughter. Birthdates of the older sons are not known; the sons are listed in the order they were named in George Murray's will. Their names were: **Alexander, James, John, George, William, David, Jacob,** and **Charles.** History about **David**, whose family line continued in Ohio and Missouri, will be found in Chapter Four, David Murray's Family in Ohio.

Family stories and posts on Ancestry.com state that the first son of George and Mary was **Alexander**, born 1765 in Reading, Pennsylvania.

Some entries on Ancestry cited Alexander's birth as 25 December, 1765, in Berks County, Pennsylvania. However, the Pennsylvania Church Records show that on that date a child was baptized by a Rev. Alexander Murray. (1)

The Parish Administrator of St. Gabriel's Episcopal Church in Berks County acknowledged by email that Rev. Alexander Murray was a minister at the church, but there were no birth or marriage records for Murray or Schneider (Snyder). No birth records for Alexander have been found.

The first proven fact about Alexander was that he married Abigail Tryon on 30 October, 1792, in the First Presbyterian Church of Goshen, Orange County, New York. Abigail was born 3 December, 1767, the daughter of Eliud Tryon and Abigail Reeve. Spencer Murray believes that George (father of Alexander) was buried on the Eliud Tryon farm. (2) One wonders why

George would be buried on the Eliud Tryon farm when Alexander was a land owner in 1793.

On 1 July, 1794, Alexander and his wife Abigail, sold seventy-six acres of land to James Murray, Alexander's brother, "which said James is now in possession of said land," for 166 pounds, thirteen shillings and four pence. Witnesses were William Murray and Mathias Keen.

Alexander was enumerated on the 1800 and 1810 census reports of Wallkill, Orange County, living in the house next to his brother William. Alexander stated his age as between 60-69 in the 1830 census, making his birthdate between 1761 and 1770. In the 1840 census he was probably living with his son-in-law, John Benedict, in Chemung County. The census report listed one male age 70-79 in the Benedict family.

Alexander was listed on the 1799 New York Tax Assessment Rolls of Real and Personal Estates 1799-1804, living in Wallkill, on a farm with real estate valued at $607 and personal property valued at $115. (3) He was listed on the same assessment roll in 1801 with a farm valued at $707 and personal property valued at $115. The reader will note that several descendants of the Murray family lived in or around Wallkill, an area originally in Ulster County and added to Orange County in 1798. This is another indication that George Murray's land, for which an original deed has not been found, was located in Wallkill.

Alexander's will was filed in Chemung County, New York. He was living with his daughter Emeline and her husband John Benedict. The will stated that Alexander left no widow. His will was written 1 April, 1844, and probated 1 June, 1847. It named children and grandchildren to receive inheritances, but his sons, Alexander, Jr. and Eliud T., were omitted; possibly they were disinherited.

Alexander, Jr. lived in Chemung County until his death in 1883. In the 1870 census of Chemung County, he stated the value of his real estate as $4500 and his personal property as $500. Eliud was enumerated in the 1850 census of Owensboro, Davies County, Kentucky where his occupation was listed as "painter."

Alex Murray

Birth: unknown
Death: Mar. 24, 1847

Inscription:
81 yr-from Orange Co. Sgt., Rev. War

Burial:
Riverside Cemetery
Chemung
Chemung County
New York, USA
Plot: Lot 60

Created by: RobMinteer57

Record added: Oct 24, 2012

Find A Grave Memorial# 99522871

Alexander Sr. was buried at Riverside Cemetery, Chemung County, New York, close to his daughter Emaline and her husband John Benedict. There is a cemetery marker recognizing him as a soldier in the American Revolution, although it seems that he would have been very young to serve in the Revolutionary War. Also, it is doubtful that he would have served as a sergeant when he was so young.

Caution is advised in researching Alexander Murray in New York because there was another Alexander Murray who lived in Newburg, Orange County, at about the same time period. Facts about the two men should be compared.

An entry on the 1799 New York Tax Assessment Roll in Newburgh, New York, listed Alexander Murray with real estate valued at $4100 and personal property valued at $750. Because he is shown on the Newburgh roll, it is doubtful that he is Alexander, son of George. There is a notation which reads: "Alexander Murray, late heirs of Alex C, (unintelligible) & Daniel Aldrich, heir of A.D." The Aldrich name could indicate a relationship to Bethia Aldrich, the second wife of Eliud Tryon; however further research will be required.

A will entry from Orange County, filed 12 April, 1803, and probated in 1812, named an Alexander Murray and wife Jane who lived in Newburgh. He, too, had a son named Alexander, Jr. More research is necessary on these two families to prove which man had the military record.

James, born ca.1767, was named as Executor of his father's will. He either died young or left Orange County after 1810.

In H.H. Vail's, *Genealogy of the Vail Family,* he stated that James married Sally Ann Vail, born 16 February, 1802, daughter of General Abraham Vail. (4) However, Sally Murray is not listed in Abraham Vail's will probated in 1851. Three daughters, Sally Ann, Almina and Eliza are named in Abraham's will, but they must have been unmarried because he listed other daughters with their married names. Therefore it seems questionable that the Sally Ann named in Vail's Genealogy married *this* James Murray.

In the 1800 census, the family of James Murray listed two males under ten and two females under ten. The 1810 census listed at least seven or eight children (or servants under twenty-five). If Sally Ann was born in 1802, she could not have been mother to these children.

On 1 July, 1794, James Murray purchased seventy-six acres in Orange County from his brother Alexander and wife Abigail. This sale was noted in the section on Alexander.

James is listed in the 1799 New York Tax Assessment Rolls in Wallkill living next to his brothers Alexander and William. James lived on a farm, real estate valued at $207 and personal property valued at $90. In 1801, James was listed only as owning personal property valued at $300. In 1802 his personal property was valued at $420.

In 1806 James purchased land from Peter Miller, Orange County, which identified James as "carpenter."

On 9 May, 1808, James Murray and his wife Susannah, town of Wallkill, sold three acres to Nathan Rasco for the sum of $276 current money of the United States. There could be a relationship to Nathan (Nathaniel) Rasco, which was not found in this research. Nathan Rasco was in the New York Militia during the War of 1812, serving in Colonel Michael Smith's Regiment, the same regiment as George and Jacob Murray. All three men were enrolled from 7 September, 1814, until 14 December, 1814.

James Murray was not found in Orange County in the 1820 census or in later census reports of Orange County.

The third son, **John**, born ca.1769, was listed in the 1799 New York Tax Assessment Rolls in Wallkill, when he was assessed for personal property with $15 value. In 1801 he was assessed for real estate valued at $50, personal property valued at $10. He was listed in the 1800 census of Wallkill, Orange County, with 1 male under 10, 1 male 26-45, 3 females under 10, and 1 female 26-45. In the 1810 census there are only five household members and in 1820 census, there is only one male under ten. John and his wife were listed as over 45 years of age.

No land transactions were found for John in Orange County.

John is named in his father's will, as well as his daughter, Eleanor. A line at the end of the will states "John's daughter excludeth from anything." It is not clear if this refers to another daughter of John, or whether Grandfather George changed his mind about his gift to Eleanor.

No other information has been found about John.

George, Jr., born ca.1771, married Esther Schultz on 22 November, 1789, at the United Methodist Church, Newburgh, Orange County. They were listed in the 1810 census of Minisink, Orange County, with 1 male 10-15 and 4 females under 10. The family was also listed in the 1820 and 1830 census, but George was not listed in the 1840 census; however his widow Esther, was found in the 1850 census.

A federal tax was imposed on United States citizens on 9 July, 1798, which required valuation of lands, dwelling houses, and slaves, when their total value exceeded $100. Documents for this tax are scarce, most lost or destroyed. A tax assessment for northern New York in Clinton County, described taxed properties in detail. For example, Pliny Moor's property was described in this way: "Owner and occupant of a wood house 40 x 30 feet, 1½ stories, seven windows, 4 x 2 ft., one 3½ by 2 ft., one 2 x 2 ft., two 3 1/3 by 1½ ft. One acre valued at $600."

George was a farmer and owned a store near Dolsontown. He was apparently taxed following imposition of this new federal law. A tax was assessed against him on 1 October, 1798, for a wood house, 35 x 27 feet, one story, no windows, value $230/$340 at the town of Deerpark, Orange County. The house stood on one acre. This raises a question. Why was it necessary to state that there were no windows? Perhaps as a frugal Scotsman (or Irishman or Englishman), George placed shutters on his windows and did not install glass windows, which would have increased the value of his home and thus his tax.

George Murray was listed in the 1799 New York Tax Assessment rolls in Deerpark, Orange County. He owned a house and farm valued at $345 and had personal property valued at $30. His tax bill was 37 cents. This would be the same location mentioned in the previous paragraph.

Esther applied for a widow's pension for George's service in the War of 1812. He served in Captain Samuel Webb's Company and was listed on the Payroll Abstracts for the New York State Militia from 07 September, 1814, to 12 December, 1814. His service was eligible for service pay of $25.33.

Children of George and Esther were Matilda, George and Thomas. George's daughter Mary was bequeathed a portion of the final settlement in her grandfather's will. Is Mary the same person as Matilda? Or did Mary, named in the will, die young?

George's son, George, operated a grocery and retail store in the town of South Centreville, Orange County. An obituary was found for the son, George W., which said that he was one of a large family of children; however names of those children have not been found.

The obituary stated that George W. opened a general country store in Centreville and later received an appointment of postmaster. He was also a farmer.

William, born in 1773, married Mary Ann Beakes. His date of death was 20 December, 1848. William and Mary Ann were buried in the Minisink Cemetery, Orange County. Their children were: Archibald Yard, Sally, Cynthia, Amelia, William M., Edmund Beakes, Ambrose Spencer, Hiram Stacey, Mary Ann, and Henry Beakes.

This family line has been researched more than any other line. Ms. Ada Murray Safford is a direct descendant of Archibald Yard Murray. (See Chapter One.)

In Ruttenber's, *History of Orange County, New York*, William was identified as a farmer, an active and influential citizen of the county and a deacon in the Baptist Church. He was a Democrat and cast an electoral vote for James K. Polk. (5)

In the 1799 Tax Roll, William was enumerated with real estate valued at $385 and personal property valued at $105. Taxes were 49 cents.

William was listed on the Wallkill tax rolls in 1803. In 1827 he was named as "Overseer of the Poor," described as an "Old School Baptist," and elsewhere as a "hard-shelled Baptist." He went into business with Stacy Beakes, Jr. and Joseph Beakes in their dry goods and grocery store. The business failed and William lost his farm, living his last years with his daughter, Amelia. (6)

William and Mary Ann's second son, William M. married Ellen Maria Matlack and followed the political interests of his father. He was elected to the United States Congress in 1850 as a Democrat and was re-elected in 1852. Quoting again from Ruttenber: "During his second term he was called upon to cast his vote on Mr. Douglas' Territorial Bill, which involved repeal of the Missouri Compromise of 1820. Mr. Murray's opposition was steady, vigorous and unyielding and his vote was cast against the Douglas bill on its final passage, and for this he was read out of the party."

The bill cited was the Kansas-Nebraska Act which repealed the Missouri Compromise of 1820 and allowed the vast area from Oklahoma to the Canadian border to admit slaves, if the residents voted in favor of slavery in their new territory. The bill resulted in bloodshed in the bordering states and was a contributing factor to the Civil War. It was sponsored by Stephen A. Douglas, and passed the House 113 to 100; Mr. Murray casting his vote with the naes.

He then participated in the organization of the Republican Party. In 1857, he became president of the Goshen Bank and remained there until his death in 1875.

Another son of William and Mary Ann was Ambrose Spencer, who became clerk of the Orange County Bank in 1831, cashier in 1834, and president from 1845 to 1867. He was a director of the Erie Railway for fourteen years and one of the directors of the Farmers Loan and Trust Company of New York. He was originally a member of the Whig Party, but when the Republican Party was organized in 1856, he became a member and was elected to the United States Congress, sitting in the seat formerly occupied by his brother William. He was elected treasurer of Orange County and served for three terms.

William M. and Ambrose Spencer were very successful in banking and business. In the 1860 census of the town of Goshen, Orange County, Ambrose S. was listed as a banker with real estate valued at $44,000 and personal property valued at $110,000.

In the nineteenth century, county histories and biographical sketches usually contained glorious descriptions of an individual. A publication, *Portrait and*

Biographical Record of Orange County, New York, contained a biographical sketch of Ambrose Spencer Murray. (7)

The author of the sketch said: "More lasting than the crumbling granite of stately monuments is the memory of generous deeds, sympathetic words and tender thoughtfulness of those who have finished life's battles and left us..." He continued his description of A.S. Murray: "He came to Goshen and entered the Orange County Bank, acting in the capacity of clerk. Here he had an opportunity to develop his business capacity and so faithful was he in the performance of every duty that he soon gained the confidence of employees and in 1834 was elected cashier. In 1845, A.S. became president of the bank and served for forty years."

In the United States Congress, heated exchanges over slavery and admission of new states as slave or free had gone on for years, peaking in severity before the Civil War broke out. Ambrose Spencer Murray was present when tempers flared in the event called, "The Caning of Charles Sumner." Earlier, in 1856, Sumner had denounced the Kansas-Nebraska Act in his "Crime against Kansas" speech. He argued for the immediate admission of Kansas as a free state. Sumner attacked the authors of the Act, Stephen A. Douglas of Illinois and Andrew Butler of South Carolina. Representative Preston Brooks, Butler's cousin was so incensed that he wanted to challenge Sumner to a duel.

Rather than a duel, Brooks chose to beat Sumner severely with his gold-topped cane. Sumner was trapped under his desk and Brooks said that he beat him across the head, neck and shoulder "to the full extent of my power." When the cane broke, he continued beating Sumner with the gold head.

Records from the House of Representatives stated that Representatives Ambrose S. Murray and Edwin B. Morgan intervened and restrained Brooks. The two escorted Sumner to the cloakroom where he received medical care. Sumner, however, was not able to return to his seat for four years due to the severity of his injuries. It was said about Ambrose Murray: "He had the name of being the strongest man in Congress, but it was really his Scotch pluck that gave him power in such cases."

During the Civil War, the Underground Railroad passed through Orange County. The Neversink Valley Museum of History and Innovation has an excellent description of routes through New York. Slaves from the south sometimes caught train rides north, usually riding on cold boxcars. Quoting from the museum history: "Some lucky passengers got to ride in heated passenger cars. A. S. Murray of Goshen, an Erie Railroad director, was a strong abolitionist. He would see to it that a pass or ticket was issued to runaways who came his way." (8)

With these illustrations, it is easy to understand why the author of the *Biographical and Portrait Record* could be so effusive in his praise of A.S. Murray.

However, as in all families, there are black sheep. William M. (cited above) and his wife Ellen had a son named William M. who became cashier at the Goshen Bank. He was twice elected treasurer of Orange County. Newspaper headlines in the early 1890s must have created quite an embarrassment for the family.

The *Middletown Daily Times*, June-July, 1892, reported that the county treasurer's books were examined and found wanting. The *Middletown Daily Times*, 22 August, 1892, printed: "Cashier Murray's shortage (Goshen Bank) is about $75,000. He is still missing and his where about is kept from the public."

The *Middletown Daily Times*, 16 July, 1892, reported that "Mrs. William Murray and her family left Goshen on train today for Elmira where they will make their home for a time with Judge Gabriel Smith, Mrs. Murray's father."

The Supreme Court of Orange County issued a judgment and foreclosure on William's property to be sold at public auction.

The 1893 *Middletown Daily News* described Murray as "absconding Treasurer of Orange County."

The *Middletown Daily Argus*, 7 December, 1897, published an obituary. "William M. Murray, formerly cashier of the Goshen National Bank and twice county treasurer of Orange County died at the State Hospital at

Binghampton, age nearly 60 years. Mrs. W.D. VanVliet of this village is his sister. Two sons and his wife survive him." Binghampton was founded in 1858 as an inebriate asylum to treat alcoholics. In 1880 it was converted to a hospital for the chronically insane.

Mary, the only daughter of George Murray and his wife Mary Jane, was born in 1774, and married Mathias Keene. A post on Ancestry.com said that Mary died 3 October, 1793. Spencer Murray said that she died seventeen days after the birth of her son, George.

The Ancestry post stated that Mathias Keene was born 9 August, 1774, and died 9 January, 1835, in Canaan, Wayne County, Pennsylvania. According to that post, Mathias Keene remarried 3 October, 1794. His wife was Anna Reeve, daughter of Deacon James Reeve.

In the 1800 Minisink, New York tax rolls, Keene was listed with real estate valued at $125 and personal property valued at $6. In the 1810 census of Minisink, Orange County, Matthias Keene (sometimes spelled Keen) was listed with 2 males under 10, 1 male 26-44, 2 females under 10, and 1 female 16-44.

In Williams' biography of Middletown, he stated that Henry Wisner and Mathias Keene operated a store on Main Street. In 1804, Keene built a house west of the church and opened a hotel, possibly the first in Middletown. Keene sold the store in 1806. Williams stated, "Husband of Anna Reeve, Keene was the father of eleven children." (6)

In the first census of Middletown, completed in 1807, Mathias Keene was listed with three males and three females in his house. This corresponds with the results in the 1810 census.

In 1792, the United States Congress passed an act to establish a uniform militia throughout the United States and in 1793 New York put this act into force.

In the *Military Minutes of the Council of Appointment 1783-1821*, Mathias

Tribute to Matthias and Anna Keen.

Keene was listed as a Lieutenant in Lt. John Wilkins Regiment, Orange County in 1808. In 1809 he was promoted to Captain of the Light Infantry. (9)

According to the Wayne County Pennsylvania Historical Society, "Captain Mathias Keen moved in 1811 to Canaan from Milford, which was then part of Wayne County and built the first dam at King's Pond. He operated a grist mill and was a public-spirited citizen who did much to develop the township and county." (10) Records of Wayne County showed that Keene/Keen ran for sheriff of the county in 1819. Final vote count was 217 for Solomon Moore and 143 for Mathias Keene.

Mathias and Anna were buried in the Keen Cemetery, Wayne County, Pennsylvania. Location is on Route 6, east of Waymart, north on Elk Lake Road, then left ¼ of a mile. Family members erected a plaque dedicated to Mathias and Anna. Their tributes revealed pertinent information about the family. The dedication to Mathias read: "A settler 1815. Founder of this cemetery. These millstones hewn by his hands from yonder Moosic, turned by waters of canoe. Keens Lake 1816."

The dedication to Anna read: "In this wilderness then known as Elk Forest, she reared thirteen children descendants of whom have erected this memorial."

The Ancestry post mentioned earlier said that Mathias and Mary had children, Jane and George William. Add the eleven mentioned in Williams' biography and the total of thirteen children would be the thirteen mentioned in the cemetery memorial.

David was born ca.1777. Information about David will be found in Chapter Four.

Jacob was born ca. 1780 and married Elizabeth Osbourne. A researcher who posted the grave site for Commodore C. Murray, stated that Commodore's parents were Jacob Murray and Elizabeth Osbourne. Another entry on Ancestry.com stated that Elizabeth first married Jacob Murray and then married Benjamin Lawson after Jacob's death. In the 1850 census of Lumberland, Sullivan County, New York, Benjamin Lawson, age 82, is listed living with Elizabeth Murray, age 68.

In 1860 census, she is listed as Elizabeth Lewson (Lawson) living with her son, C.C. Murray and his family in Tusten, Sullivan County, New York. Her tombstone is in Glen Cove Cemetery, Sullivan County, New York. She died 8 April, 1866, at the age of eighty-four years. Her son Commodore and his wife Lucinda Corwin Murray, are also buried there.

Jacob was a member of the Mt. Moriah Masonic Lodge No.189 in Wallkill, Orange County, New York. In the 1809 enumeration, Mathias Keen was listed as Senior Warden, Jacob Murray was Junior Warden. Charles and William Murray were listed as members.

Payroll abstracts for the War of 1812, New York State Militia, lists Jacob Murray as Q.M. Sergeant serving in Col. Michael Smith's Regiment. He was paid $38.40 for his service from 7 September, 1814 to 12 December, 1814. This is the same time period when his brother George served.

In the 1830 census of Thompson, Sullivan County, New York, Jacob Murray was listed as a male 40-49; Elizabeth was listed as female 40-49. There were three males under 19 and three females under 19. One female was listed in the 20-29 age group. She could be a daughter or a servant. Jacob was not found in the 1840 census, but Elizabeth was listed in the 1850 census as being in the same household as Benjamin Lawson.

Jacob's son, Commodore C. Murray, served as Supervisor for the town of Tusten 1859-64 and 1866-70. The obituary on Find a Grave stated that Commodore was a merchant, hotel owner, large land owner and influential man in Tusten. He built the Murray Hotel which was the second one opened to the railroad public when the rail was finished.

Charles was born 11 October, 1782, and died 25 January, 1834, in Washtenaw County, Michigan. He married Abigail Reeve 23 December, 1810, in Orange County. He was town clerk of Deerpark 1815-1817. In 1804, he sold the land

Commodore C. Murray

Birth:	1814
	Otisville
	Orange County
	New York, USA
Death:	Feb. 3, 1884
	Narrowsburg
	Sullivan County
	New York, USA

Commodore C. Murray
Born in 1814 in Otisville, Orange County, NY the son of Jacob Murray and Elizabeth Osbourne. He was a Merchant, a Hotel owner, large land owner and influential man in the Town of Tusten. He married Lucinda Corwin born in 1820 and died 12 March 1893. According to the New York State Census records for Tusten their children were; Jane Frances; Walter C. (who died in Civil War in VA); Richard W.; Commodore Harrison; Charles J (who married Lucy Schryver); Delphine A. (who married Freeling Tufts); and George W. (who died in 1855 at age 2 years.) He built the Murray Hotel which was the second one opened to the Rail Road public when the rail house was finished to Binghamton. This eating house later owned by his sons C.J. and C.H. closed in the spring of 1888. C.C. Murray (as he was better known) was Town of Tusten Supervisor1859 to 1864, also from 1866 to 1870. It was in this home in July 1839 that the Methodists held their first meeting.

Family links:
Parents:
Elizabeth Osbourn Lawson (1781 - 1866)

Spouse:
Lucinda Corwin Murray (1816 - 1893)*

Children:
Walter C Murray (1841 - 1862)*
Commodore Harrison Murray (1845 - 1926)*
Charles J. Murray (1848 - 1936)*
Delphine A. Murray Tufts (1851 - 1943)*
George W. Murray (1855 - 1855)*

Siblings:
Elizabeth Murray Drake (1805 - 1891)*
Commodore C. Murray (1814 - 1884)
Cynthia Murray Williams (1816 - 1888)*

Find A Grave Memorial# 39506906

—Mr. C. C. Murray, familarly known as Commodore Murray, for nearly half a century a prominent resident of Narrowsburg, after a long and severe illness, passed away about 7 o'clock on Sunday evening last. His death was peaceful. He was favored with long life, having nearly completed three-score and ten years, and during his long residence at Narrowsburg he was closely identified with the development of this region of country. Doubtless a multitude of friends as they receive this intelligence, will pay at least a silent memorial tribute. The evening of his life was passed in close communion with his Bible and his God, in almost constant prayer and devotion. May the kind, heavenly Father mitigate the severity of this stroke to the stricken family!

Wayne County Herald, Honesdale, PA
February 7, 1884

he inherited from his father, to his brother William. In 1830 he moved his family to Washtenaw County, Michigan.

From the *Portrait and Biographical Album of Washtenaw County Michigan*: "He settled on section 10, taking up eighty acres of land from the Government for which he paid $1.25 per acre. The old house built by him on coming to the place still stands, and it was probably the only frame house in the township at the time of its erection." (11)

Also from *Portrait and Biographical Album:* "His son, William C, was known as among the well-known and influential citizens of Superior Township—using the best methods of fertilizing and improving the land." William C. was born 1824 in Orange County, New York.

c J.E. Witkowski

Charles Murray

Birth: Oct. 11, 1782
Death: Jan. 25, 1834

Family links:
Spouse:
Abigail Reeves Murray (1793 - 1878)

Children:
William Conklin Murray (1824 - 1908)*

*Calculated relationship

Inscription:
BORN AT ORANGE CO. N. Y.

Burial:
Pray Cemetery
Superior
Washtenaw County
Michgan, USA

Created by: Laura
Record added: Jan 01, 2006

Find A Grave Memorial# 12840717

William Conklin Murray and his parents were buried in Pray Cemetery, Superior Township, Washtenaw County, Michigan.

After reviewing estimated birthdates of George's children, one wonders if Mary Jane was a minor when she married George. Or, perhaps their marriage was delayed while George recuperated from his war injuries. Alexander was born in 1765 and the other children's births were approximately two years apart until Charles was born in 1782. The spacing of their births was common in colonial days. It further questions their marriage date of 1756.

Bibliography

(1) Pennsylvania Church Records, Adams, Berks and Lancaster Counties 1729-1881. Found on Ancestry.com.

(2) Murray, Spencer. *"One American Branch of the Scottish Highland Clan Murray."* Private copy.

(3) New York Tax Assessment Rolls of Real and Personal Estates 1799-1804. Found on Ancestry.com.

(4) Vail, H.H. *Genealogy of the Vail Family.* New York: DiVinne Press, 1902.

(5) Ruttenber, E.M. and Clark, L.H. *History of Orange County, New York.* Philadelphia: Everts & Peck, 1881.

(6) Williams, Franklin B. *Middletown, a Biography.* Middletown, New York: Lawrence A. Toepp, 1928.

(7) *Portrait and Biographical Record of Orange County, New York.* New York: Chapman Publishing Co., 1895.

(8) Neversink Valley Museum of History and Innovation, 26 Hoag Road, Cuddleback, New York, 12729.

(9) *Military Minutes of the Council of Appointment.* Volume II, 1783-1821. New York. Found on Ancestry.com.

(10) Wayne County Historical Society, 810 Main Street, Honesdale, PA 18431.

(11) *Portrait and Biographical Album of Washtenaw County Michigan.* Chicago: Biographical Publishing Company, 1891.

4

David Murray's Family in Ohio

David, the sixth son of George Murray, was born ca.1777. He married Mary Hulse, born 14 September, 1787. She was the daughter of Jonas and Hepzibah Reeve Hulse, a descendant of the Reeve/Hulse families who lived on Long Island prior to the Revolutionary War. Mary's brother, Jonas, married Cynthia Murray, daughter of William and Mary Ann Murray. (See Chapter Three.)

Deacon James Reeve came from Long Island about 1763 and settled on a farm in the Wayawanda Patent. He was one of the principal men who were instrumental in building the First Congregational Church of Middletown, Orange County. Deacon Reeve was married two times and had a total of eighteen children. His daughter, Anna, from his first marriage, married Matthias Keene after Keene's wife, Mary Murray, died in 1793. Hepzibah's mother, Mary Moore, was Deacon James' second wife, making Anna and Hepzibah half-sisters.

The first census of the United States was taken in 1790. George Murray had three males under sixteen living in his house. This would confirm the minority status of David, Jacob and Charles. David's name did not appear in the 1800 census, probably because he was not a head of family. He could have been living with his brother William, because on 10 November, 1798, David sold his 1/3 interest in the fifty-six acres he inherited to his brother William. (1) This would indicate that David sold his interest in the farm when he became twenty-one. His brothers, Jacob and Charles, sold their interests when they reached majority.

David appeared in the 1801 New York Tax Assessment Rolls living in Wallkill, assessed for $130 in personal property. By 1803, his assets had increased to $150 taxable personal property.

David was married between 1801 and 1810 because on the 1810 census of Minisink, David's household listed 2 males under 10, 1 male 26-44, 1 female under 10, and 2 females 16-25. No record has been found of his marriage and no record has been found of these three children. The second female in the 16-25 age group could have been a relative or servant.

According to the "Deerpark Diary," when the town of Deerpark was established in 1798, the town council created a highway commission and nineteen road districts. (2) Each district had a road master or overseer. The highway commissioners determined how many work days would be needed in order to maintain a road in good and passable condition. Road overseers organized work crews provided by adjacent land owners and saw that each person performed the necessary work. If an owner was unable to work, the overseer hired a worker and added the cost to the taxes of the owner. David was Road Overseer in 1808, 1809, and 1810, and registered his cattle mark 5 November, 1810.

On 7 April, 1809, David purchased two pieces of land from Nathaniel Kimber for $2250. The land described was part of the Wayawanda Patent, lying on the west side of the drowned lands, containing one hundred thirty-four acres. (3) The Wayawanda Patent originally incorporated most of Orange County; unfortunately there are few descriptions in the deeds identifying where the properties were specifically located or the names of adjoining land owners.

Ruttenber's *History of Orange County, New York*, listed families residing in school districts in Minisink between the years of 1810-1815. In District #6, he named David Murray and one tenant, as well as James Hulse, who was probably the same James Hulse found later with David in Pickaway County, Ohio. James Hulse was Mary Hulse Murray's brother.

On 3 July, 1816, David Murray and his wife, Mary, sold one hundred forty-four acres to Jesse Wells and William Wells for $2375. This land was in the town of Deerpark, Orange County, formerly in Ulster County, but changed to Orange County in 1798. (4)

The only children of David and Mary that can be documented are Hepzibah, born 1 March, 1812, in Orange County, Nancy Jane, born 1813 in Orange County, David Caton, born 16 October, 1822, in Pickaway County, Ohio, and Zelotes G., born 5 June, 1825, in Ohio.

The proof that Hepzibah was the daughter of David and Mary is the inscription on her tombstone in the old Wallkill Cemetery. It says: "Hepzibah Murray, age 13, death 1 May, 1825, granddaughter of Jonas Hulse." Jonas and Hepzibah had only one daughter who married a Murray, and the name Hepzibah occurs frequently in the Hulse/Reeve families. This raises the question: Why did Hepzibah stay in New York when her family traveled to Ohio? Was she ill or disabled? This question will probably remain unanswered.

There are no records for David and Mary Murray after they sold their land in Orange County in 1816, until they were listed in the 1820 census of Pickaway County, Ohio. In the 1820 census of Pickaway County, David's family consisted of 1 male under 10, 1 male 10 to 15, 1 male 26-45, 3 females under 10, and 1 female 26-45. Nancy Jane would have been one of the females for she was born in 1813 in New York, as confirmed in later census reports. No information has been found about the other two daughters and two sons.

David and his brother, Charles, left Orange County to travel west and it is possible that James and John may have left also. Individuals looked for good land and opportunities available in the western lands after the War of 1812.

Charles, however, went to Michigan, as did Archibald Yard, the son of David's brother, William. Ohio records indicated it was the Hulse family, not the Murray family, that convinced David and Mary to move to Ohio.

Pickaway County, Ohio, was formed in 1810. The name came from Piqua, which was the name of a Shawnee tribe. Circleville became the county seat. An article from the *Olive Branch and Pickaway Herald*, quoted by Van Cleaf, explained the advantages of Circleville: …"25 miles south of Columbus and 20 miles southwest of Lancaster…It is on the most direct route from Philadelphia and Washington City to Cincinnati and Illinois; on which route the public mail destined for those parts now passes in stages to and fro three times per week and is soon expected to pass daily." (5)

James R. Hulse, Mary's brother, went to Pickaway County and the Ohio wilderness in 1811, coming with all he possessed tied in a pack on his back. He was a wheelwright by trade. On 17 May, 1812, he married Rebecca Van Meter in Pickaway County. She was the daughter of early settler Isaac Van Meter, who left Rebecca $1586.66 in his will. Since anyone who possessed more than $1000 was considered wealthy in those days, Rebecca's inheritance must have provided a comfortable nest egg for the family. James was a Mason, a member of Pickaway Lodge #23. According to Van Cleaf, James R. Hulse acquired over 3,000 acres and was considered quite prominent in Pickaway County.

Mary's brothers, Silas and Israel, as well as her sister, Martha, also came to Ohio in the early 1800s. Mary and her siblings were confirmed as living in Ohio when their father, Jonas Hulse, made his will and distributed inheritances to his children.

However, it remains a puzzle as to what happened to David and the children named in the 1820 census. He was alive until 1825 when Zelotus was born. Perhaps there was an epidemic which claimed their lives? According to the

History of Pickaway County, "1826 was a hard year for pioneers of Jackson Township. An epidemic called 'the cold plague' caused the death of many people." (5) There was also a widespread cholera epidemic in 1830. In addition, life in the wilderness was full of dangers—Indians, wild animals and accidents.

The next puzzle is why did Mary leave Pickaway County and travel north to what was then Crawford County? Van Cleaf quoted from the newspaper again, "The town (Circleville) contains one hundred and two dwelling houses …the population consists of one hundred and seven families…The public buildings are a court house, jail, a building containing six public offices, an Academy, a public schoolhouse, a Presbyterian church and a market house." Why did she choose to leave her brother, and the civilization described by Van Cleaf?

She may have been convinced to move by her brother Silas, who had already settled in Crawford County. She may have wanted to leave the county where she had experienced so much sadness. Or, perhaps her brother Israel, wanted to move to a county where government lands were available at $1.25 an acre; he may have wanted to establish his trade as a surveyor.

Mary was listed in the 1830 census of Crawford County, Ohio. She was named as head of the household with 2 males 5-10, 1 male 20-30, and one female 30-40. The two youngest boys are David and Zelotus; the older male is quite possibly Mary's brother, Israel Hulse. He never married and had close personal and financial ties with Mary. It is doubtful that the male could have been one of Mary's other sons because there was no Murray male listed in the 1840 or 1850 Ohio census that would appear to be Mary's son. Also, Israel Hulse does not appear as a "head of a family," in the 1830 or 1840 census, indicating that he did not have a separate household.

John A. Morrison and Nancy Jane were living close by, identified on the census report with 1 male 20-30 and 1 female 15-20. They must have been recently married because there were no children listed.

Silas Hulse (Mary's brother) and family were living next door, although his name was spelled as "Cyles Hults," on the census report. His family consisted of 4 males under the age of 5, 1 male 30-39, and 1 female 20-29. Other names which were found as Murray neighbors and later appeared in Wyandot County were Doctor Dunn, Robert Gibson and Josiah Gibson.

Crawford County was organized in 1820, named after Colonel William Crawford, who had been savagely killed by the Indians in 1782. As years passed the whites and Indians lived together, not always peacefully, but, in general, they respected the rights of each other. A description of their interactions was found in *The History of Wyandot County*: "The Delawares as well as the Wyandots, when journeying from their reservations in search of game, almost invariably stopped at all the houses of the white settlers, and when they came to a white man's cabin, expected to receive the hospitality of the inmates; if they did not, they were much offended. They would never accept a bed to sleep upon; all that was necessary was to have a good back-log on, and a few extra pieces of wood nearby, especially in cold weather for them to put on the fire when needed. They usually carried their blankets, and would spread them upon the floor before the fire; and give no further trouble. Often they would leave those who had sheltered them a saddle of venison or some other commodity which they had to spare." (6)

The area would have been a wilderness when Mary and her brothers arrived. What a change from New York. Men cleared the land by cutting down large trees, clearing the underbrush and breaking the ground so that food could be grown to sustain the family until the next growing season. They next constructed a small cabin from logs and used stones to erect a chimney. Neighbors could erect a small cabin in two or three days, but the occupants had to finish the inside walls and erect simple beds and tables. According to *The History of Wyandot County*, almost every farmer had a patch of from one quarter to one half an acre planted with flax. After the flax was harvested and prepared for spinning, women spun the flax and wove it into bedding and clothing. Both men and women wore the product: pants, shirts and skirts of "linsey-woolsey."

How did Mary settle her land without a husband and with two boys under ten? Perhaps Israel helped her and maybe her brother Silas; perhaps her neighbors and son-in-law pitched in too. Silas' sons would have been too young to work like men, just as Mary's young sons were too young. How did she subsist? She must have been a very strong woman to survive physically and emotionally without a husband. But she did. And she began acquiring property.

On 10 December, 1826, a land patent was issued to Jonas Hulse of Ohio for Section 31, Township 1 South, Range 14 in the district of lands offered for sale at Delaware, Ohio, containing 105 acres. It is doubtful that Jonas traveled to Ohio to make application; one of the children must have applied for it in his name. One wonders if Jonas bought the land to help Silas and Mary establish their families in the new county.

On 1 November, 1828, Jonas and Hepzibah Hulse sold to Mary Murray, of the town of Tymochtee, county of Crawford, fifty-one acres in Section 31, Township 1, Range 14, being a part of a tract of land which Jonas Hulse purchased from the United States. It is suspected that Jonas sold the other half of this parcel to his son, Silas. In *The History of Wyandot County*, Silas Hulse's heirs were listed as early owners of real estate in Section 31, owning fifty-six acres. It also indicates that Mary moved to Crawford County soon after her husband's death.

On 25 October, 1833, Mary Murray sold Silas three acres, being a tract of land which Mary purchased from Jonas. The land described began at the middle of the county road west of John Morrison's house and to the land owned by Doctor Dunn.

On 14 May, 1835, Mary Murray sold to Israel Hulse the east ½ of the west section of Section 31, Township 1, Range 14, beginning at a road from Tymochtee Creek, the land owned by Mary Murray and running between the land of Mary Murray and Silas Hulse, deceased. Early land records named Mary and Silas, John Morrison and Doctor Dunn, who were all settlers listed in 1830 census of Tymochtee Township.

In April 1836, Mary purchased two pieces of property obtained by patent from the United States government. Certificate #12906 confirmed a purchase of eighty acres in Section 13, Township 2, Range 12 and certificate #12907 confirmed a purchase of forty acres in the same section, range and township.

Mary sold the forty acres which she obtained on patent #12907 to her son-in-law, John A. Morrison on 12 July, 1837. John A. Morrison was the first teacher in the township and was later named when the Star Bethel Church of God met in the Morrison Schoolhouse, located in Richland Township. (6) John was probably the teacher for David and Zelotus at the Morrison Schoolhouse. Leggett has another entry listing Israel Hulse as a teacher.

In the 1840 census of Hancock County, Bucyrus Township, Mary Murray was listed as head of the household, age 50-60, with 1 male 10-15, 1 male 15-20, and 1 male 30-40. This shows the same relationship as in the 1830 census and seems to confirm that Israel was continuing to live with Mary. It may be confusing to read the names of different counties where Mary was enumerated. Crawford was established in 1820 and Hancock County lost land to Wyandot County when Wyandot was created in 1845. Hancock, Delaware, Hardin, and Marion changed boundary lines until the creation of Wyandot.

On 7 July, 1842, Israel Hulse wrote his will. He asked that James R. Hulse of Pickaway County serve as his executor and that his sister, Mary Murray, receive all his movable property. He gave his niece, Nancy Jane Morrison, forty acres of land on Section 31, Range 13, and gave all his surveying apparatus to his nephew, Aristeus (son of James R.). He gave to two of his nephews, Caton and Zelotus Murray, forty acres in Section 14, Range 12. He gave a piece of land on Section 31, Range 14, to Albert Hulse, where Albert's father (Silas) was buried. The last 120 acres were to be sold to pay his debts, and if there was an excess, after the land was sold, that amount was to be given to his brother, Ambrose, in New York. The 120 acres were sold to James P. Ward, whose son, Alfonso, married Rubirta, daughter of Z.G. Murray in 1872.

This will confirmed family relationships between the Hulse family and Mary Murray. It also revealed the name of Israel's nephew, Caton, which was the middle name for David C. Murray. That name was not known by the family until this will was found. A family member in Ohio said that Zelotus' middle name was Grindel. This may be correct because his grandson was christened Zelotus Grindel. He only used "G." as his middle name in all public documents. The will also indicated that Israel was a surveyor, a vocation much in demand when settlers were staking their claims and boundaries. Surveyors frequently purchased lands for their own speculation, which may explain why the lands named in his will had all been purchased from the United States government.

As more settlers poured into Ohio, the United States government made plans to move Indian tribes further west. The remaining tribe in what became Wyandot County was the Wyandot tribe that signed a treaty accepting a tract of 148,000 acres west of the Mississippi River. The tribe was promised annuities plus two blacksmiths, a blacksmith shop, steel, iron and tools, an agent and an interpreter. The final result was less than the original treaty; however in the spring and summer of 1843, the Wyandots began their move west. "The parting scenes at Upper Sandusky were most affecting. Consultations were held in the council house, and religious worship in the church, almost constantly for days before the final departure. The last resting places of loved ones were tenderly cared for." (6) By this time, most of the Wyandots had been Christianized and one of their leaders, Grey Eyes, was an ordained Methodist minister. Regardless of this, they were forced to move.

Following the establishment of Wyandot County in 1845, John A. Morrison was elected recorder. He was re-elected in 1848, but was defeated in 1851 for clerk of the court. He was one of the sureties on the performance bond to build the courthouse in 1846. John ran for probate judge in the October, 1861 election, but was defeated.

The *Wyandot Democrat* ran an endorsement for John on 15 August, 1861. "Our nominee for Judge is well known in the county—is a pleasant and agreeable gentleman, with rare qualifications for the office. He was the first county recorder for Wyandot County; has the reputation of being the best penman in this part of Ohio, is posted in the law, and is an active, careful businessman—just the man for the position."

Some of the first owners of real estate in Richland Township were Mary Murray, John Morrison, and Israel Hulse. C.D. Murray was listed as owner of personal property. This is probably an error and should have read D.C. Murray.

On 17 August, 1847, Mary sold sixty acres for $200 to David Murray. The land description was Section 13, Township 2, Range 12. On 5 May, 1849, Mary sold twenty acres to Zelotus, located in the same section, township and range. These transactions indicate that Mary was beginning to pass her land to her two sons. This divided eighty acres between the sons, but there is no indication why David received more land than Zelotus.

Zelotus married Nancy Benjamin on 2 December, 1846. In the 1850 census of Wyandot County, he is listed as Zelots G. Murray, age 26. Also in the family were Nancy age 23, William B. age 2 and Effa M. age 1.

David Murray married Susannah Long on 18 January, 1849, in Wyandot County. David was listed in the 1850 census, living three houses away from Zelotus. He was age 28, Susannah was age 20 and Jerima (Jerema) was age 1. Mary Murray, age 62, was also in the household when this census was taken 14 September, 1850.

On 28 October, the census taker visited John Morrison's household. His census report read: John A. Morrison age 42, schoolmaster; Nancy J. age 39, Cinderella age 18, Hannah age 14, J.H. age 11 (male), John S. age 9, Mary E. age 7, James B. age 3, and Mary Murray age 68. This would indicate that Mary was enumerated twice. She may have been moving between families, although she does not appear in the Z.G. Murray household in any census report. This could also indicate a problem which is evident later in this narrative.

On 5 May, 1849, David and Susannah Murray sold 40 acres to Zelotus Murray located Section 14, Township 2, Range 12.

On 11 January, 1854, John A. Morrison and Nancy Jane sold eighty acres to David Murray, located in Section 13, Township 2, Range 12. Z.G. Murray, as justice of the peace, examined Nancy Jane regarding her dower rights.

On 7 September, 1855, David Murray sold to Zelotus twenty acres of land in Section 13, Township 2, Range 12.

David and Susannah had two more children: Isaiah, born 1850 and Ezenith, born 1853. Susannah died sometime after Ezenith's birth because on 13 December, 1855, David married Huldah Mariah Doud in the city of Adrian, Salem Township, Wyandot County. He was thirty-two; she was sixteen.

Huldah was the daughter of Owen Doud and Harriet Higbie Doud. Legget notes that the Star Bethel Church of God first met in the fall of 1854 at the Morrison Schoolhouse. The membership numbered eleven souls, two of whom were Mr. and Mrs. Dowed. (6) It seems very probable they were Huldah's parents and David met her at a church meeting.

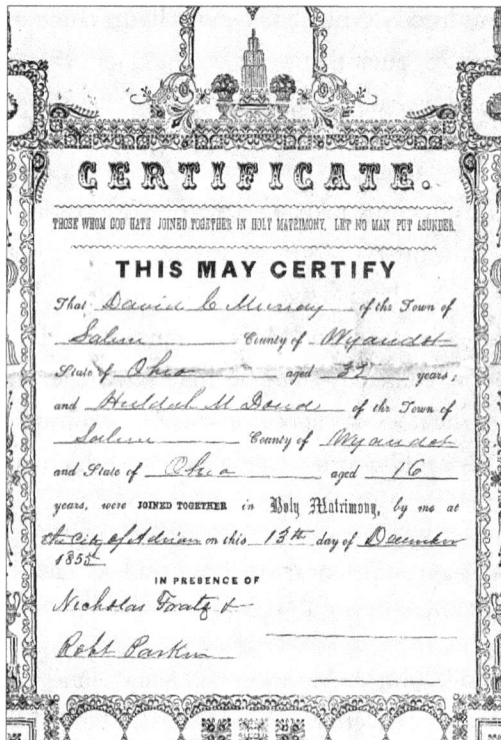

Marriage certificate for David and Huldah.

Harriet Higbie Doud was the daughter of Flemmen and Sally Higbie, originally of New York. Sally wrote a little book on handmade paper listing the names of her siblings and their birthdates, as well as the names of her children. That book was passed to her daughter Huldah.

Harriet wrote the names of her siblings.

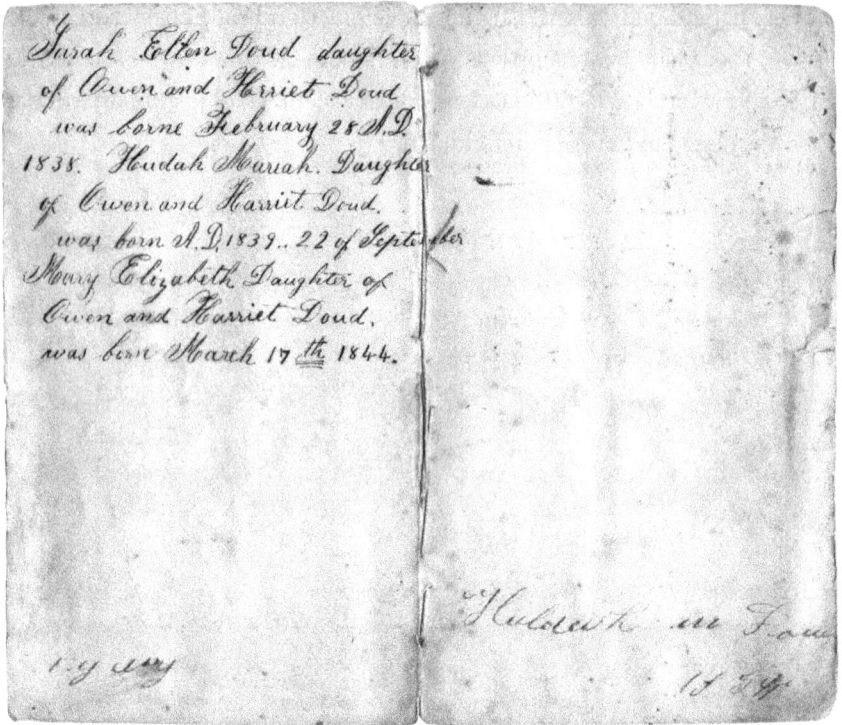

Harriet wrote the names of her children.

Harriet wrote the birthdates of her three daughters, the only children of Harriet Higbie Doud and Owen Doud. No information has been learned about Sarah Ellen, except reference to her children in a letter from Mary Elizabeth (Aunt Moll) to her nephew, Z.G. Murray, in Springfield, Missouri, written in 1906. (See Chapter Nine.)

Harriet also wrote names and birthdates of her brothers and sisters, a genealogy list comparable to those found in a family Bible. Owen and Harriet were married 13 April, 1837, in Knox County, Ohio. Their family is listed on the 1840 census, with two females under five. Owen is not listed in the 1850 census reports in Ohio.

Harriet's grave was shown on Find a Grave, Ancestry.com, buried in Bethlehem Cemetery, Lima, Ohio. No date of death was given, but the researcher noted w/o Owen Doud. No other records have been found about Owen Doud.

David was listed in the 1860 census of Salem Township, Wyandot County. He was age thirty-five, living with Huldah, age twenty, and children Jerema, Isaiah, Ezenith and Jasper P., age two. The print is so faint that it is very difficult to read and the census taker misspelled the daughters' names, but this is our David.

Also living in Salem Township was John A. Morrison age 52, Nancy age 47, John W. age 18, Mary E. age 16, James R. age 12, Doctor M. age 9, and Samuel J. age 5.

Z.G. and Nancy lived in adjoining township of Richland (shown on census as T.G.). He was age 36, Nancy age 33, William R. age 13, Effa M. age 11, Reuberta age 7, and Emma age 5. There is an error on Z.G.'s age. He is two years younger than David.

Conspicuously missing in the 1860 census is Mary Murray. She is not found living in the household of any of her children. One could easily assume that she had died and there would be no further record of her.

Nancy Jane Morrison died in 1861. An obituary in the *Wyandot Democratic Union,* published 15 August, 1861, said that she died on the 11th after a short illness. The only other notation was: "Nancy Jane, wife of John A. Morison, aged 48 years, 8 months, and 17 days." No survivors were listed.

*Gravestone for
Nancy Jane Morrison
found in the Old
Mission Cemetery.*

There is a stone for Nancy in the Old Mission Cemetery, Upper Sandusky, which said that she was born in 1813 and died in 1861. On 2 June, 1863, John appeared in probate court to apply as guardian for his children, James R. age 16, Doctor J. age 11 and Samuel J. age 9. There are no papers or letters to indicate family contact after Nancy died. John was not found in later census reports of Wyandot County; he either moved on or died.

There is also a stone in the Old Mission Cemetery for a child named David C. Murray, born 1863, died 1864. One wonders if this could be David and Huldah's child. David and Huldah had four more children after Jasper was born in 1858. Zelotus G. was born in 1861, Andrew Jackson was born in 1865, William was born in 1867 and Evalene was born in 1869. The birth and death of David C. could fit between the births of Zelotus and Andrew. It is unusual that David C. would be buried in the Old Mission Cemetery since there was a graveyard on David's farm. And yet, there were only two known Murray brothers in Wyandot County at this time.

Following are notes collected by David in 1857 which were the earliest papers found with David Murray's signature. These notes may have been made by individuals needing money during the Panic of '57.

David and Z.G. were respected community leaders. They loaned money, collected money for others and acted as guardians and administrators of estates. On two of the documents, David signed his name with "J.P." indicating that he was a justice of the peace.

David Murray was elected treasurer of Wyandot County in October, 1861. He defeated his Republican opponent by 255 votes. The *Wyandot Democrat* newspaper wrote an endorsement August 15, 1861: "David C. Murray. Our candidate for Treasurer has resided for many years in Salem Township, is highly respected and esteemed by all who knew him; and we need no greater assurance of his integrity and uprightness as a man, than the popularity and reputation he has won for himself in the western part of the county. Well qualified for the position, and a safe, careful and accurate man, he will make an excellent Treasurer."

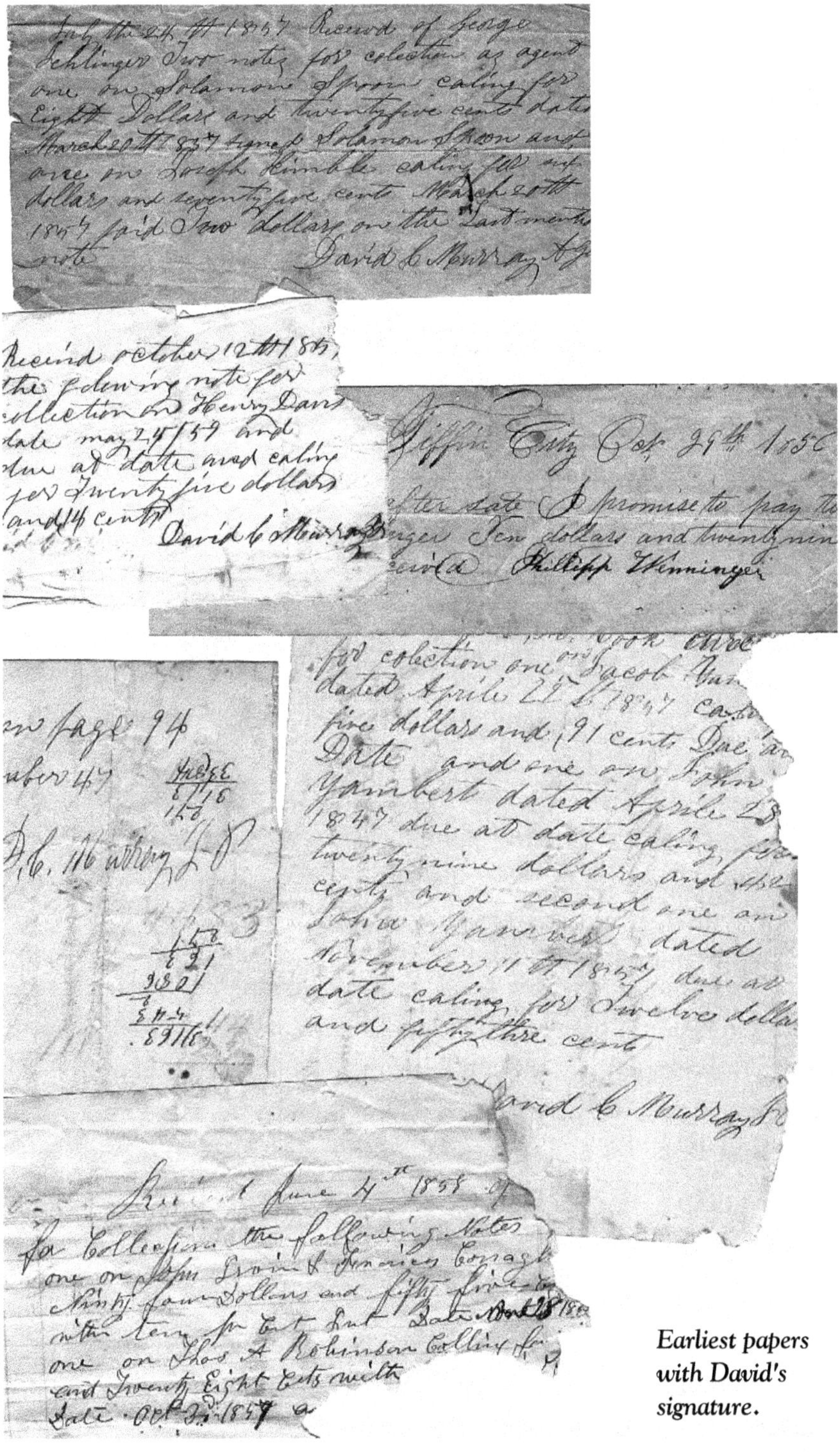

Earliest papers
with David's
signature.

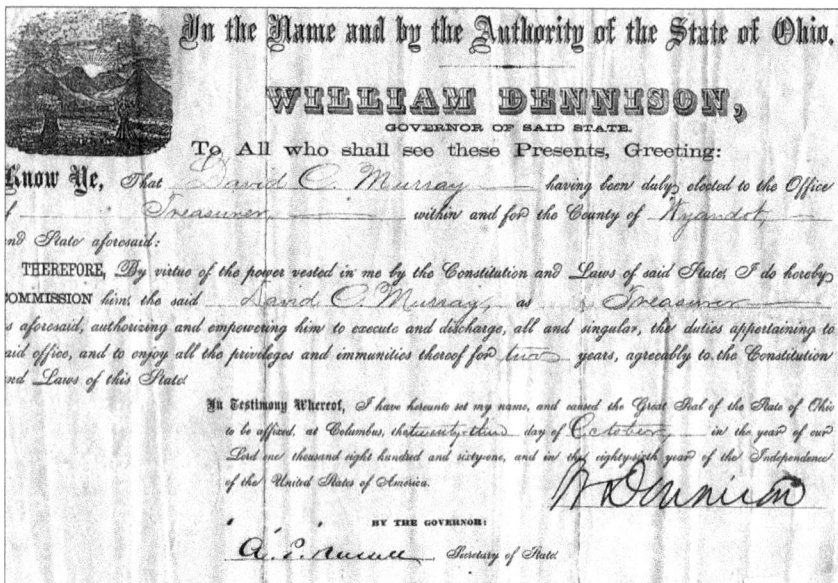

David elected treasurer of Wyandot County.

He was re-elected in October, 1863, defeating his Republican opponent by 100 votes. Leggett states that David was elected county commissioner in October 1868, although David was already living in Missouri by this date. (6) Z.G. was elected treasurer of the township of Whartonsburg 1865-68 and justice of the peace in 1869. These two Murray sons were following the political paths of their relatives in New York.

There was one difference however. David and Zelotus were Democrats; the Murrays in New York were Republicans. William, brother of David's father, left the Democratic Party after his dissenting vote on the Kansas-Nebraska Act, the act which further extended slavery into the western territory. The Republican Party was formed in reaction to slavery, while the Democratic Party, considered the party of the South and supporters of slavery, continued in its conservative views. One of their standard bearers, Andrew Jackson, must have impressed David C. because he named his son, Andrew Jackson.

The *Democratic Pioneer* was organized 12 September, 1845, in Upper Sandusky, with the statement printed that it was to be thoroughly Democratic. The editor said, "Every Democrat in Wyandot and surrounding counties, is constituted an agent, to get at least one good subscriber." Zelotus' letters frequently discussed Democratic and Republican candidates and squabbles between the two parties.

In January 1865, David sued for partition of land belonging to the dower of Barbara Long, widow of Joseph Long, with proceeds to be divided between the heirs. Some of the heirs were Jerema Murray, Isaiah Murray and Ezenith Murray, confirming that Susannah Long, their mother, was the child of Barbara and Joseph. The land in question was located in Section 20, Township 2, Range 13, and advertised in the *Democratic Union* for public sale. David bought the eighty acres for $1500. Proceeds were distributed to the heirs, less $80 paid to the attorney.

Although nothing has been found to prove that David was a member of the Masonic Order, there were three funeral notices found in his Bible. Two of them announced that the deceased would receive Masonic honors. It would be plausible to believe that David was a Mason since his uncles in New York were Masons, as well as his uncle James Hulse in Pickaway County and his brother-in-law, John Morrison.

Funeral notices found in David's Bible.

David served as treasurer of Wyandot County during the Civil War. His military registration was found showing his age and occupation. Possibly because he was forty-one and an office holder, he was exempt from service. Ezenith Murray Sell told her daughter, Jerema Dixon, that David rode the train to Columbus, carrying money for the soldiers, dressed as a tramp so that he would not be robbed.

Civil War registration.

Ohio passed a militia bill on 28 May, 1864, which required the assessor to enroll all male citizens between the ages of eighteen and forty-five, at the time they were assessed for personal property. Those serving were to perform military duties in volunteer companies, essentially the same as a National Guard. Those declining to serve had to pay a four dollar commutation fee to the county treasurer by the 15th day of August each year. As treasurer of the county, David collected the fines which were paid into a military fund.

Examples of fines imposed and receipt for payment of fines. These were obtained from the Assessor's Office in Wyandot County.

There are no family stories indicating why David decided to move to Missouri, but apparently he started planning his move about a year before he left.

It could have been that he read newspaper articles which encouraged people to move to Missouri. In the 12 April, 1866, edition of the *Springfield Weekly Patriot*, there is an article reprinted from the *New York Tribune* extolling the virtues of Missouri: "The future of Missouri must be glorious. No other state presents so many and so varied attractions…All this point men of small means as well as men of capital and enterprise to Missouri." Newspapers posted stories about twenty to thirty wagons moving through their towns every day, headed west.

On 6 September, 1866, David turned in his books and accounts to the county of Wyandot and received the following receipt: "Received of

Receipt from treasurer's office.

David C. Murray the sum of Eighteen Thousand Eight Hundred and Seventy four Dollars, Ninety one Cents, Nine Mills, balance in full of all funds due Wyandot County at that date together with all books, and papers belonging to the treasurer's office of said county."

On 13 August, 1867, David and Huldah sold 200 acres to their neighbor, George Kear, for $7150, except 1/8 acres on side of the tract in Section 13, Township 2, Range 12, "being now enclosed and used for burying purposes." There is a strong possibility that Susannah was buried there. A neighbor stated that the gravestones were used as flooring in the new owner's barn. There is no verification for this story. (There is a reference to this graveyard in a letter from Aunt Moll which will be found in Chapter Nine, Zelotus Murray's Family).

The *Democratic Union Wyandot* newspaper published the following editorial on 22 August, 1867: "Personal. Our esteemed friend, D.C. Murray, Esq. started, with his family, on last Monday, for his new home in the West, five miles from Springfield, Mo. We, in common with the citizens of this county, regret exceedingly to part with the Squire, for he was one of our most influential citizens. We truly hope he may find his new home pleasant, profitable and agreeable to all his expectations."

With that, David Murray left Ohio, never to return.

David and Zelotus corresponded until David's death in 1872 and some of Zelotus' letters were saved in the family trunk. But—no letter was saved which dealt with the death of Mary Murray.

Bibliography

(1) Deed Book I, pages 328, 329. Orange County, New York.

(2) "Deerpark Diary," Town of Deerpark Historian's Office, Huguenot, New York. March 2008.

(3) Deed Book L, page 361. Orange County, New York.

(4) Deed Book R, page 414. Orange County, New York

(5) Van Cleaf, Aaron R. *History of Pickaway County Ohio.* Chicago, Illinois: Biographical Publishing Company, 1906.

(6) *The History of Wyandot County.* Chicago, Illinois: Leggett, Conaway & Co., 1881.

5

What Happened to Mary Murray

Ezenith Murray's daughter remembered her mother saying that Mary died in a fire in an old folks' home. As in many family stories, there are kernels of truth in the stories, but they are not totally accurate. There were no "old folks' homes" in the 1860s. Spencer Murray had printed Mary's date of death as 18 November, 1868. Since no family member in Missouri knew Mary's date of death, it was obvious that a family member in New York had learned about her death. Was there an obituary? Not in Wyandot County. However, the Wyandot County newspapers and the *Ohio Statesman* ran headlines that answered that question.

The *Wyandot Democratic Union* published an article on 26 November, 1868, re-printed from the *Ohio Statesman* newspaper. The headline said: "DESTRUCTION OF THE LUNATIC ASYLUM."

The Lunatic Asylum of Ohio was organized by an act of the General Assembly on 5 March, 1835. The directors selected a tract of land very close to the State House in Columbus, erecting a building at a cost of $61,000. On the evening of 18 November, 1868, a fire originated in the northeast wing of the building, a section occupied entirely by women. There were three hundred fourteen patients in the asylum, which housed both deaf and insane.

The *Ohio Statesman* reported: "There were six of the female patients who died of suffocation and inhalation of the flames. They were placed on mattresses on the piazza, near the main entrance, and afterwards conveyed to the dead house in the North Graveyard to await the orders of their friends. Their names and residences are: Mary Murray, Wyandot County; Susan A. Parker, Licking County; Bridget Brophy, Columbus; Clara Bradford, Lizzie Herrold and Caroline Conner, Athens County."

Because Mary was a patient at the state lunatic asylum, it is not surprising that the family did not speak or write about her. With so little known about mental illness in the nineteenth century, families were embarrassed when a loved one was placed in an institution.

According to records obtained from the Ohio Historical Society, Mary Murray was admitted as patient #4453, on 11 July, 1865. The record stated that she was a widow, age 78, a Baptist and of Wyandot County. Her place of birth was left blank. In the remarks section, there were these: "In case Mrs. Murray dies she is to be buried here and her son D.C. Murray of Springfield, Missouri is to pay all expenses. Clothing will be supplyed [sic] by friends." (1) It is strange that there was no mention of Z.G. since he lived in Ohio and one might think that he would visit her and supply his mother with clothing.

The rules of the asylum required paying patients to post a bond. The regulations read: "On entering the Institution, they are required to pay for three months in advance, and to give bond and security for the punctual payment of all expenses thereafter, monthly in advance. And to remove all doubt in regard of the security, their solvency must be established by a certificate from the Clerk of the Court, or prosecuting Attorney of the proper county."

For the paying patients, the Superintendent could receive them when there was room for them in the institution and after he received a certificate signed by two respectable physicians. The price of boarding, washing, medicine and attendance for a paying patient was fixed at $3 per week. They were to furnish their own clothing, which was to be, "well assorted, neat and substantial, and in sufficient quantity." (2)

The notation in Mary's record confirmed that she was a paying patient, not an indigent sent there after trial by a court confirming her insanity. Bowling Green University is the repository for early Wyandot County records. (3) Their research staff found no Wyandot probate court records or bonds pertaining to Mary Murray. This would indicate that she did not have a court hearing and her case was kept out of the public eye. David was serving as county treasurer at that time; it would be easy for him to arrange her commitment with a friend at the court house.

In the 1850 census, Mary was living with David and then Nancy. Was she difficult to manage and moved back and forth between the families? With no mention of her name in the 1860 census, was she living in a back room with her family that did not want her listed on the census as insane?

Medical records, such as they were, could not be released from the Ohio Historical Society records due to privacy laws. From the Patient Record Books, Series 896, common causes of institutionalization for women were: religious excitement, spirit rapping or puerperal mania. The latter could be a diagnosis for younger women with post-partum depression, but who knows what behaviors could lead to the diagnosis for the other two causes. In the twenty-first century, I think Mary would have more likely been diagnosed with senile dementia or Alzheimer's disease. Several female descendants on the David Murray line have had some form of dementia.

The files stated that Mary was buried in the Circular Cemetery on the grounds of the state institution, but no one at the Ohio Historical Society knew its location. A site on the internet called, "Franklin County Gravestone Photos, Franklin County, Ohio," showed Mary's gravesite. The person compiling the photos, Leona Gustafson, stated, "The cemetery has no name that I am aware of. I call it Asylum #1 because there are three such cemeteries in close proximity. There are approximately 311 graves. It can be seen to the south of 1-70 eastbound."

Mary's grave is in a circle of graves. Going clockwise around the circle, she is #9. This is a new stone and probably was placed there at a later date when Mary's body was moved from the original site on the asylum grounds.

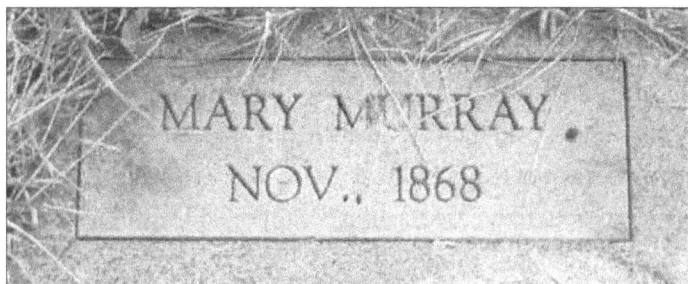

*Mary Hulse Murray. Photo copied from
a tintype, date unknown.*

What a sad ending for a woman who endured so much. As a widow, she moved to the Ohio wilderness in 1830, purchased and settled the land while raising her two young sons. The boys studied at a nearby school house and became literate. She sold her land to them so that they could become financially independent. Hopefully, they appreciated her sacrifices.

Bibliography

(1) "Record Series List 1176, Columbus State Hospital." Ohio Historical Society, 1985 Velma Avenue, Columbus, Ohio 43211.

(2) By-Laws, Rules & Regulations for the Government of Ohio Lunatic Asylum, Acts of the General Assembly, 1840. Found on Internet Archive.

(3) Bowling Green University, Center for Archival Collections, Bowling Green, Ohio 43403.

David C. Murray from a tintype, date unknown.

6

David C. Murray in Greene County, Missouri

At the end of August, 1867, David and his wife Huldah, his daughter Ezenith, their sons Jasper, Zelotus, Andrew and William, boarded a train in Upper Sandusky, Wyandot County, Ohio, bound for Greene County, Missouri. Jerema Sell Dixon remembered that her mother Ezenith told her they lost little Andrew in St. Louis. Imagine looking for a two-year-old in the chaos of people and animals as they changed trains. Luckily they found him before the train left or they would have been forced to go on without him.

Rail lines were only partially finished across central Missouri. In 1858 the westernmost extension had been completed to Tipton and by 1861 it was extended as far as Sedalia, but further building was put on hold until after the Civil War. Fortunes rose as small towns became home to a railway station and fell as the rails moved to a new location. The author of the *History of Pettus County, Missouri*, recalled: "In 1860, the then thriving railroad termini, first Tipton, then Syracuse, then Otterville and Smithton were crowded with wagons of every description, and with goods in immense quantity brought there by railroad, and taken thence by wagon trains to the west and southwest." (1)

David and Huldah traveled as far as Sedalia. After the family left the train, they continued for five days, hiding at night and watching for bushwhackers, who were still raiding and terrifying citizens in Missouri after the Civil War.

The most direct route to Springfield was the old Boonville Road, used by the Butterfield Overland Mail as it crossed Missouri on its way to California. When John Butterfield planned his mail route in 1858, he established stations along the route for a change of horses and for travelers to partake of food and water. Although the Butterfield Overland Mail Route lasted only two years, some of the station locations persisted in the years following. Perhaps the Murray family stopped at one of those for simple refreshment.

The route through Cole Camp, Warsaw and Bolivar led to the cabin occupied by Tapley Daniel and his family, located between Little Sac River and Little Dry Sac River. The last station before the Overland Mail stopped in Springfield was Evans' Station, located just two sections north of Daniel's home.

What did Huldah think when she saw the Daniel's log cabin, knowing this would be her new home, while remembering that she left her two story brick house in Ohio? The children may have viewed their trip as an adventure, but did David and Huldah see it as a change in lifestyle?

Tapley Daniel moved to Greene County from Tennessee around 1846. Soon after, he set about acquiring real estate, sometimes buying from other early settlers; at other times obtaining land grants from the United States government. Two receipts show 120 acres in Section 26 purchased in 1846 for $1.25 per acre; another receipt shows 40 acres in Section 35 purchased in 1855 for $2.50 per acre.

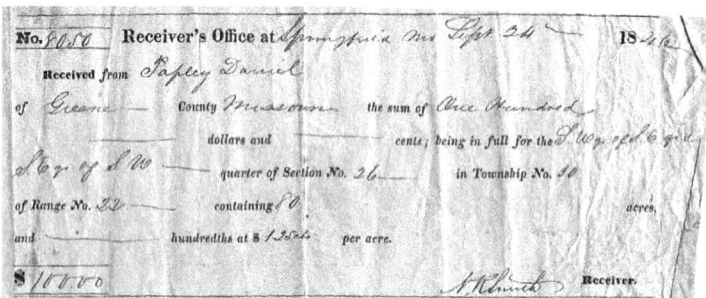

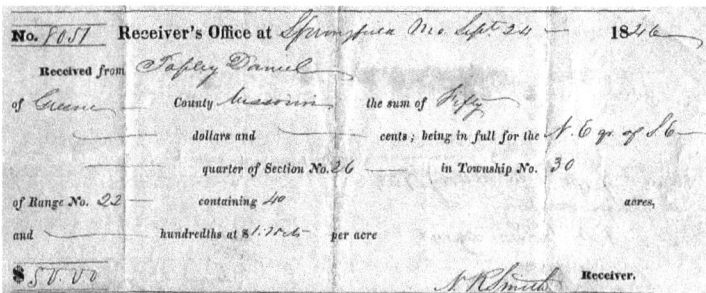

He put together contiguous parcels for a total of 320 acres located in Sections 26 and 35 which he sold to David on 5 September, 1867. Soon after the sale was completed, Tapley and his wife, Keziah, moved to Miller County, Missouri with their daughter Lucinda and her husband Giles Williams. There are no records to show how the men became acquainted, but letters from Tapley to David indicated a friendly relationship.

The right side was torn off in the following letter written in October 1868. It was a puzzle to understand why Tapley was referring to Col. John Phelps until the court case of Daniel vs. Banfield was found in the Greene County Archives. John Phelps had returned to the practice of law following his service during the Civil War and apparently was representing Tapley in a civil law suit. Colonel Phelps was a highly regarded lawyer in Springfield and was elected Governor of Missouri in 1876. This letter sounded like a response to depositions relating to the case and indicated that Tapley couldn't make it to Springfield because of bad weather.

This is the background for the case. The Confederate Army occupied Greene County for two short months in early 1862 and during that time, soldiers and those sympathetic to their cause, quickly confiscated property belonging to Union supporters. When General Sterling Price and his troops fled to

Letter from Tapley Daniel referring to Col. John Phelps.

Arkansas, many Greene County Confederate sympathizers left with them. It is probable that Tapley's son, John, as well as Tapley's son-in-law, Joseph B. White, were in that group.

The court system barely operated during the Civil War and cases were brought to court after the Civil War when Union citizens sued to have their property returned to them.

In July, 1865, Qualls Banfield sued John Daniel for wrongfully taking his horse valued at $135 and his clothing valued at $40. (The date of taking the horse and clothing were not in the court record.) Those being sued (the Confederates) could not appear in court because they knew nothing about their cases and the property was returned to the previous (rightful) owners. The Banfields were ardent Unionists and this probably was the cause of their disagreement. The court ordered the sale of two mares and a filly with the proceeds to go to Banfield.

In 1866, Tapley filed suit against Qualls Banfield and Sheriff Patterson for wrongfully taking his horses. Tapley argued that the horses were his, not John's. John swore that he took his horses with him when he left the state. Lucinda Daniel Giles swore that the horses were her father's horses.

Letter from Tapley asking for compromise in the lawsuit.

In 1871 Tapley wrote to David, "I want you and Hardy White to settle that case if it takes all...." The letter was repaired with tape and what followed is not readable.

Records indicated that the case was finally settled out of court with costs assigned to the defendants (Banfield and Patterson). In May of 1871 Tapley said he was satisfied with the compromise. "Pay yourself and send me the rest," he instructed. The letters indicated that David was involved in the compromise and out of court settlement. See story of the Banfield family in *Butterfield Overland Mail—Early Settlers in Northern Greene County.* (2)

David was comfortable working in arbitration because his name frequently appeared in Wyandot County court records. Tapley must have been satisfied with David's compromise because he closed the letter with, "your true friend as ever."

Letter from Tapley stating he was satisfied with the compromise.

Rocky mount Miller Coo Mo

June 12 1871

Mr Murray my friend i take my
pen in hand to drop you a few
lines to let you no we are all
well and hope when this came
to hand it will find you all
well i am not a needing that
money and you can use it as
see proper if you dont want to
pay that money to stop the interest
i dont want to recieve any more
untill due when ever you
want to pay any money to stop
the interest i will recieve it
i wrote you a letter some time
a go i guess you have got it i am
very well satisfied about that
settlement between me and
Banfield i will close i remain
your true friend as ever

yours tauley tapley Daniel

D C Murray

Tapley stated again that he was satisfied with the compromise.

Greene Co Mo Dec 27th 1870

Esteemed friend in Answer to the
within I drop you A few lines
we are all well and was pleased
hear that you was well allso
I aske you a letter some time
back and Ask do you what you
would discount on the note
which you sent to Hardy which
I carried Hardy tity to by

hundred dollars now I supose
you would drop so as to make
my money draw me ten per cent
I can git 12 per cent but
if you drop so as to mak me
ten per cent you can have the
money thare $600 due the 5th of
Januay and one hundred of that
is intrust which dont draw you
eny intrust which put at ten

Tapley offers to discount interest for early annual payment on loan.

Tapley Daniel bought and sold property while he lived in Greene County, turning a profit on the sales. The 1870 census of Miller County showed him living close to his daughter Lucinda with his occupation as retired merchant. His profitable investments indicated that he was an entrepreneur. The above letter shows his desire to make a little more money on his interest.

Above is a letter of condolence from Tapley to
Huldah Murray expressing his sorrow after hearing
about her husband's death.

David paid $6000 for 320 acres. Down payment was $2500 with seven installments to follow at $500 per year, interest six percent. Tapley made quite a profit on his investment, since he had acquired some of the land at $1.25 and $2.50 an acre. Local newspapers were advertising good farm land for $10 to $15 per acre, yet David paid $18.75 per acre. This is an unanswered puzzle. Why did David, so experienced in real estate sales, overpay for his farmland? His payment schedule was listed on separate pieces of paper stapled together.

Annual payment schedule.

Warranty deed between
Tapley and David.

Why did David Murray move his family from Ohio to Missouri? A relative in Ohio said that he moved to a warmer climate because of his poor health. Another mentioned that he wanted a farm ideal for raising horses. Or, perhaps it was the lure of cheap land further west.

Shortly after the Civil War, people became interested in moving west. They scouted newspapers for investment opportunities. In the *Springfield Missouri Weekly Patriot*, September 1865, J.H. Creighton and Sons, real estate agents, were advertising the sale of property in Greene County. J.H. Creighton stated that he was "late of Ohio." Perhaps David learned about land for sale in Greene County from an advertisement in an Ohio newspaper.

In several of the letters which Z.G. wrote to David, he mentioned names of neighbors who were going west, to Kansas, Nebraska and Indian Territory.

David received a letter in 1870 from an old friend asking about land in Greene County. He wrote, "I want to visit your place this winter if nothing happens to prevent me and I just thought I would bother you with a few questions. Is there still an opening in Springfield for a good or possible atty. like myself, or is it full. What can good unimproved lands be bought for....I have been in Kansas City for the last eight months but have not moved my family yet. I have some boys and want to get some land for them near where I aim to make my final house...I want eventually to turn my attention to the stock business and I want to get the best climate, water, etc. for that purpose." He describes land he owns in Kansas and Iowa which he wants to trade for land in southwest Missouri. He asks, "What kind of winters do you have and how long do you have to feed. Is your country a blue grass region naturally? How are times financially in this place? How is business, on the wane, or brisk? I think we are on eve of a money crunch and I look for very hard times akin to those of '57." He then requests David to send him a long letter answering his questions. Signed A.M. Jackson.

Note that the letter was addressed to D.C. Murray, Esq., a designation used for men who had financial standing and prestige in the community.

There are no indications about the response which Mr. Jackson may have received; however, he was prescient in his prediction of an upcoming panic, for it occurred in 1873. The hard times of '57 which he referred to in his letter were indeed the Panic of '57.

The '57 Panic occurred after the expansion of the United States economy

Many things that I dislike.

I went eventually to turn my attention to the stock business and I want to get the best climate, water, &c for that purpose

I own 320 acres of land in Anderson County Kansas which is located for a fine stock farm good land. I also own 160 acres in Ringgold Co. Iowa within one half miles of Mt. Ayr the County seat. which must be very valuable as soon as that R R is complete This is one of the finest Counties of land in Iowa and in the best climate in Iowa I would like to exchange these lands for lands in South western Missouri if I should come there. What do you suppose would be the price for a trade of this kind? What kind of mules do you have, and how long do you generally have to feed. Is your country a blue grass region naturally &c &c

How are times financially this fall, How is business, on the wane, or brisk. I think men are on the eve of a money crash & I look for very hard times akin to those of /57, How are rents in Springfield If I'm asking too much will you please write me a good long epistle touching the things herein referred to. Hoping this may find yourself and family enjoying health and prosperity I am Yours

D. M. Jackson

during the Gold Rush and the Mexican War. In August 1857, the Ohio Life Insurance and Trust Company failed and the effect rippled to other New York banks. British investors removed funds from United States banks, grain prices fell due to the end of the Crimean War, and land speculation programs that depended on rail routes fizzled.

Another factor was that the Dred Scott decision by the Supreme Court deepened the divide between North and South and caused the east-west railroad bonds to plummet.

William Murray, David's cousin, who had vehemently opposed the Kansas-Nebraska Act of 1854 permitting slavery in the western lands, must have foreseen the consequences of the act. It repealed the Missouri Compromise, caused border wars in the West, inflamed the public and stoked the fires of war.

Perhaps the most catastrophic occurrence in 1857 was the sinking of the *USS Central America*. After the banks failed, people began withdrawing their money. The United States government ordered 30,000 pounds of gold shipped from San Francisco to New York to shore up the banks. Unfortunately the ship and its cargo, plus 426 passengers and crew went down in a hurricane off the coast of Cape Hatteras, North Carolina in September, 1857.

The Panic leveled off with the beginning of the Civil War and was not as devastating as the Panic of 1873.

David had four young sons and perhaps, he, too, wanted opportunities and land for his sons. His father moved to Ohio when land opened for settlement after the War of 1812. However one wonders if his purchase in Greene County lived up to his expectations. He sold his 200 acre farm in Richland Township, Wyandot County, located on gently rolling land with dark, loamy soil. Richland Township was so named because of its rich soil. David moved to a farm located on a river bottom, which was hilly and covered with rocks.

A letter from Z.G. in September 1871 said, "Hamilton (David's son-in-law), has just returned (to Ohio) and he does not fancy your country much. He thinks it is pretty stony. Says your new wagon will soon want tyres." In the same letter, Z.G. says, "Bogart wanted to know of me if it was a fact that you had to haul wood to town for a living. I could not tell them certain, so just drop them a line; it would relieve them of doubt." These concerns make one wonder if life in Missouri went as well as David had hoped.

David and Huldah left a two story, brick Italianate house in Ohio. They began their life in Missouri living in a cabin vacated by the Daniel family. Early maps show a residence located on the curve of the road between the two rivers. A map which David must have received showed Section 35, with the two rivers, a house, and names of adjoining property owners. Homes are indicated by dark squares. It also confirms Boonville Road passing in front of the Murray home.

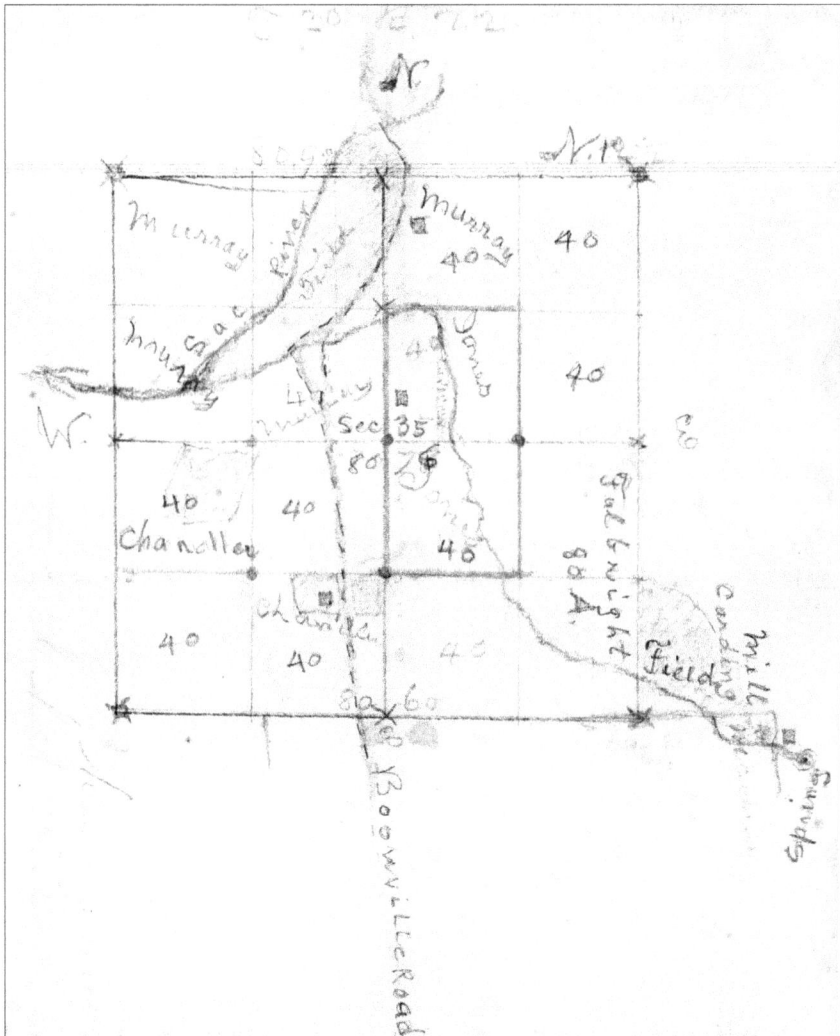

David Murray Map 1867

David Murray paid property taxes 1868-72 as verified by Missouri and the Greene County Collector's Office. It was interesting to note that in 1868 he paid a $1 poll tax; apparently that tax was eliminated in future tax years.

In those days, an overseer was appointed by the county court, who contacted landowners to work on their section of the road. If the landowner was unable to work, the overseer found someone to do the job and billed the landowner for their labor. David was given credit for services performed by a substitute. His young sons were not old enough to work and David may have been too ill. One hand worked two days for a total of two dollars.

David bought one door, two sash and lumber in November 1870 or 1871. Maybe they were for repairs to his house.

Photograph of David with one of his sons. Because it was not a tintype and his suit is of a later period, the boy would either be Andrew or William.

In 1871, David received a letter from Josiah Gibson in Wyandot County. Apparently David had asked Josiah about payment on a note transacted in Wyandot County. Josiah believed that he had paid the interest and David did not have a record of receiving the payment. This is another example of notes due David which were still being collected after he left Wyandot County. Josiah also thanked David for "helping the boys get along with their spring work." This would indicate that Josiah's sons came to Greene County.

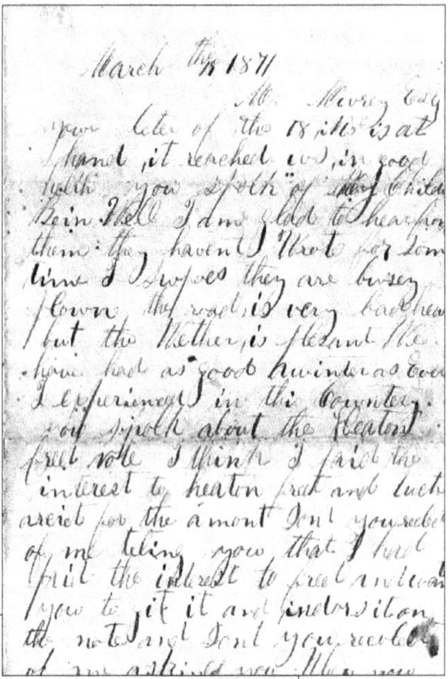

Letter from Josiah Gibson.

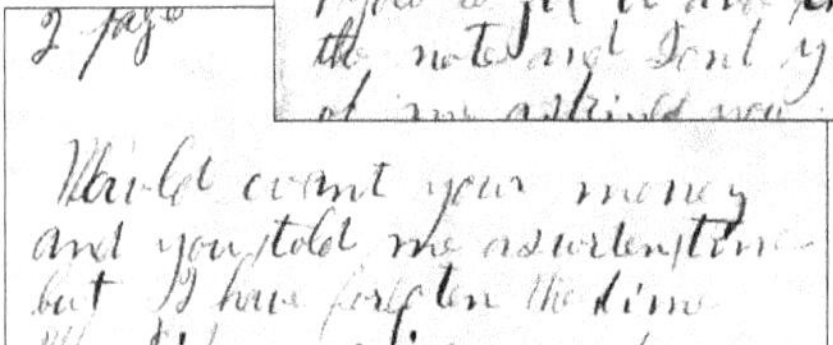

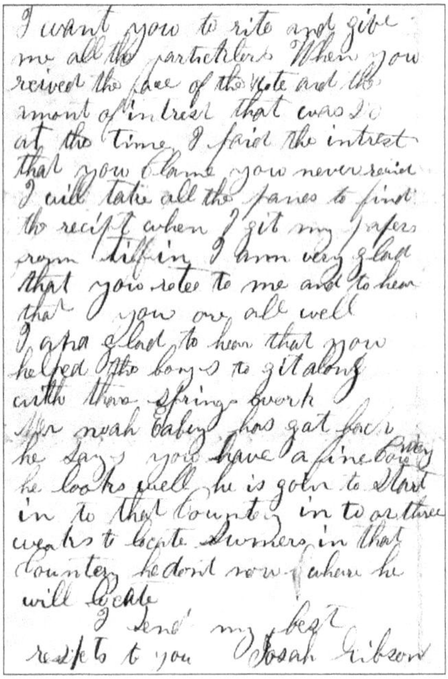

Another of the Old Pioneers Gone·

DIED—At his residence in Tymochtee township, on Thursday, Aug. 29th, 1878, Josiah Gibson, one of the oldest and most respected residents in the township.

Mr. Gibson was born June 30th, 1811, in Pickaway county, Ohio, and came to the vicinity of Tymochtee, this county, in 1822, being one among the very earliest settlers of this county. At that time, what is now Wyandot county was attached to Delaware county, and Crawford, Tymochtee and Sycamore townships, and the Wyandot Reservation was Crawford township. There were not 20 white families in the whole territory, hence he had to endure all the hardships and privations incident to that period. He was a man of great en-

Left: Obituary for Josiah Gibson.
He would have been living in Tymochtee when Mary Murray moved there. See Chapter Four.

Below: Payment to doctor for daughter Evaline.

Above is an obituary from an Ohio paper posted on Find A Grave regarding the death of Josiah Gibson. It confirms that the early Josiah Gibson was originally from Pickaway County and settled in Crawford County around the time when Mary Hulse Murray and her brothers settled there. There were references to Josiah and Robert Gibson in Z.G. Murray's letters from Ohio which indicated a family connection for many years.

David and Huldah's only daughter, Evaline, was born November, 1869. Her Texas death certificate gave her date of birth as 1873, but she was enumerated in the 1870 census showing that she was six months old. In February, 1870, Dr. Schult acknowledged receipt of five dollars in full payment of medical account for daughter. This payment could have been for services when the child was born or for services shortly after. This is confirmation of her correct birthdate; the Texas death certificate information was incorrectly provided by her daughter, Marie.

Whartonsburg Ohio
August 16/71

Friend Murry I received your
Letter and was glad to Learn
that you were all well
and doing well my self
and family are well the
neighbors are all well with
the exception Nalie Shane
She is Sick with th— art
Disease I seen uncle Jake to
Day and him and all his folk
are well I think there is a
little better crops there this
Season in Wyandot county
than ever seen before Wheat
Corn oats potatoes and every thing
Wheat worth $1.05 oats 25 ct corn
50 ct Potatoes 30 and 35 cts Stock
is cheap with the exception
of Sheep Stock hogs are worth
3 and 3½ Stock Sheep 2 and 2½
Smoked Hams from 16 to 17 for lb
I Have got 8 Head of Horses
22 Head of Cattle and 16 Head
of Hogs and 18 Sheep I
made the most money on
a little lot of Sheep I
Said 37 Dollars and 25 ct for
44 Head and Kept them
About a year and Sold
them for $160.25 I got
4 Stud Colts Said to be
the Best in Salem Township
1/2 year old 1 yearling and
2 Sucking Colts I had 25
Acres of Wheat out and it
was all good wheat I have
Not Thrashed yet I cut 18
Acres of Clover and 8 Acres of
timothy I have got 32 Acres
of corn out on my Land and
I find Part of it is very
Heavy We have had a
very growing Season every
thing Done well with the
exception of a few meadow
it is very dry here at the
present that there man
that left Missouri with
this boy Pony traded it
off before he got here for
a Set of Harness George
Kear and family are well
and is Doing well he had
out about 13 Acres
of wheat and thrashed
3,3?1 Bushels Caleb Bland
and Jacob Mosier is Running
A Threshing Machine this
fall Hughey Michaels Woman
left him about the last
of June and he has not
heard from her as far as
I know of yet John Graner
Was working at the Saw
mill got his leg mashed so
bad that it had to be
Taken off Zane George
and all the getting to be
considerable help Zane
plowed some corn he has
a young colt that he
leads around every place
with a halter
With this I will with our
Respects to S E Murr and
famil
                    D Bland

Letter from neighbor D. Bland.

David received a letter from D. Bland, in Whartonsburg, August, 1871, telling him about the old neighbors and prices of wheat, oats, cattle and sheep. He said that he had four stud colts said to be the best in Salem Township. Also he mentioned an Uncle Jake, who could be a relative, or it could be the name for an old-timer in the county.

In the 1880 census, Dwain Bland was living on a farm next to George Kear's farm, the same farm that David sold to Kear in 1867.

In 1871, David received a letter from J.H. McDonald, of Lebanon, Missouri, who apparently was writing concerning a religious publication. He wrote about trying to get minutes printed and not having money on hand to pay for them.

Letter from J.H. McDonald.

He reported that "God has blessed us with three accessions to our church since the Association, but has deprived us of our dear old Brother Elisha Turner. He died triumphant and went home rejoicing." He concluded his letter by saying, "Remember me to the Brethren and let me hear from you." This indicates a religious affiliation, although there were no family stories about David and his family attending a neighborhood church. David's Bible contained the three funeral notices noted in Chapter Four; however there was no family information. The book consisted of Psalms and the New Testament only.

In 1871, David and a neighbor, Samuel Austin, purchased forty acres in Section 26 from the Pacific Railroad Company. The railroad companies had earlier purchased land for proposed rail routes across the United States and when they were no longer needed, the companies sold the land to private individuals. The forty acres purchased by Murray and Austin were to be divided equally between the parties. The land had been purchased in the name of David Murray, who would obtain the deed when full payment was made in 1873.

Receipt from Sappington's Pills.

There is a return receipt for Dr. Sappington's Pills purchased in 1868. The receipt from Sappington's representative indicated that David may have been selling the pills and he requested credit for those unsold. Sappington's Pills were advertised as anti-fever and ague pills, but the price of one dollar per box seems expensive for drugs in 1868.

The story of Sappington's Pills is intriguing. Dr. John Sappington came to Missouri in 1819 and settled in Arrow Rock, located on the Missouri River. Because settlers traveled rivers to their destinations, they frequently were bitten by mosquitos and developed malaria. Was it possible that David's ill health, which seemed to last for several years, could have been malaria? The illness caused fever, chills and sweats, sometimes so severe that sufferers begged to die. Some individuals could have recurrent malaria attacks for years; it depended on the type of mosquito that had bitten them.

Dr. Sappington heard that quinine could help patients recover from malaria, and in some cases, prevent the occurrence of the disease. Sappington sent his son east to acquire 100 ounces of quinine, but the boy brought back 100 pounds of quinine. With so much quinine on hand, Sappington sent his children, servants and relatives to sell the pills that he was manufacturing. The medicine was so successful that Sappington later hired salesmen to go up and down the Mississippi River and through Ohio, Missouri and the South to market his pills. He made a fortune and his descendants continued the business long after his death.

Following is an example of contracts with various people in Missouri counties who were selling Sappington's Pills. The first column refers to Sappington's Pills, the second to Price's pills and the third to an amount of cholera drops. Apparently not all sellers could afford the cost of all the pills assigned to them, and they signed a note for payment to Sappington.

Person's Names.	Front 1	Residence.	Amt. of Note.	Amt. of S. Pills Rec't.	Amt. of P. Pills Rec't.	Amt. of P. Chol. Drops
John C. Goodwin		Cooper County		11.25	3.00	2.
E. L. Porter		Morgan same		30.00	3.00	2.
David Bogar		same		22.50	3.00	-
And. McFarland		Miller		56.25	4.20	3.
Cummings & Howl		same		45.00	6.60	2.
Fenley & Short		same	aug 5/1856 10.30 of	37.50	4.00	2.
Wm Coughran		" miller		1.00	.90	3.
Wm Mathews		Pulaski		30.00	4.50	1.
John B. Duncan		Maries		73.42	22.50	4.50	3.
Isaac Love		same		37.50	4.50	-
B. Nichors		Phelps		44.25	3.00	-
James W. Watkins		Dent	× 7.87	30.00	9.00	4.
Same for Howle		same	P 24.50	"	"	
Benj Corbsey		same	10.45	60.00	6.60	1.
John Godbey		Crawford	P "	30.75	2.85	4.
Wm H. Summers		Washington	"	75.00	1.80	-
Richard Summers		same	× "	94.50	5.40	5.
F. Reslop		same	"	13.50	"	-
S. S. Cory		same	"	79.50	2.25	1.
same for J. Wolf		same Bel. dew	"	3.75	1.05	3.
Murray Hale		St Francis	"	22.50	3.00	5.
C. Hart		same	3 "	30.00	3.60	4.
M. P. Cayce		same	"	22.50	1.95	4.
S. K. Pears & Co.		same	"	37.50	3.00	5.
George W. Sebastian		same	11.13	30.00	4.50	3.
C. Cox & Son		Madison	"	10.50	"	"
John Ellis		same	"	30.00	3.75	4.
Jacob Knight		Cape G.	"	12.75	.60	
J. E. Averill		Scott	"	37.50	1.35	2.
A. G. English		same	"	21.00	2.25	5.
Francis Kirkpatrick		same	"	75.00	15.00	5.
Wm F. Moore		New Madrid	"	18.75	6.00	5.

Contracts to sell Sappington's Pills.

Following is a contract completed in 1857 between E.D. and W.B. Sappington and a salesman for them with a commission allowed of thirty three and one third percent. These pills were sold for fifty cents so they may have been other than the anti-fever and ague pills, but it illustrates the widespread sales network of the Sappington Company. (All references to the Sappington Company were obtained from the Missouri Historical Society.)

David had receipts for other medicines, some of which may have been for his children. A bill was presented by A. Coyle in February, 1871, for 2 dozen boxes of American Vegetable Bilious Pills, 6 rolls of Egyptian Salve or Rheumatic Plaster and ½ dozen Worm Lozenges. The bill from A. Coyle was signed on the back showing payment of four dollars on 25 February, 1871, and for payment in full of two dollars on 27 February, 1872. A final bill in April, 1872, was for two dollars and twenty-five cents to L.M. Rainey & Co. for medicine.

These medicines do not sound like they are treatment for someone seriously ill, but on 7 April, 1872, David Murray made his last will and testament. Several of Z.G.'s letters referenced David's poor health and David may have considered making an earlier will, for a half piece of paper containing the beginning of a will was found which showed the date of 7 February, 1872.

He gave all his property to his wife Huldah during her natural life and after her death to his children: Jasper, Zelotus, Andrew J., William and Evalena. Jerema Sterling, Azenath A. Sell and Isaiah Murray, children of his first wife, were to receive $100 each, the sums to be paid from a promissory note due from George Kear of Wyandot County Ohio for $700, due in 1875.

David's wife, Huldah was appointed as sole executrix of the estate. He authorized her to sell the land in Section 26, Township 30, Range 22, which had been purchased by David Murray and Samuel Austin. He also directed that his minor children were to have a home on the farm with his wife during their minority.

I, David C. Murray of the County of Green and State of Missouri do make and publish this my last will and testament.

First: I give and devise unto my beloved wife Huldah M. Murray all and every my messuages tenements and hereditaments with all the appurtenances whereof I am seized, situate and being in the county of Green and State of Missouri, aforesaid to have and to hold all and every the messuages land, tenements and hereditaments with all the appurtenances thereto belonging, to her the Huldah M. Murry, my said wife, during her natural life, and after her death to my children by my said wife Huldah M. Murry viz. Jasper Murray, Zelotes G Murry, Andy J Murry, William Murry and Everlena Murry in equal parts in fee simple.

Second: I give and bequeath to my daughters Jerema Sterling and Azenath A Sell and to my son Isaiah Murray, children by my first wife, each the sum of one hundred dollars, which said several sums, I hereby direct shall be paid out of the proceeds of a certain promissory note executed to me by one G.W.Kear of Wyandotte County in the State of Ohio, for about Seven hundred Dollars & due in the year AD1875.

Third and lastly: I give and bequeath to my said wife Huldah M. Murry all the rest and residue and remainder of my personal estate whatsoever, after the payment of my just debts, including expenses of my last sickness and funeral.

Fourth: I hereby appoint my said wife sole executrix of this my last will and testament.

Fifth: I hereby commit the guardianship of all my minor children until they shall attain the age of twenty one years respectively, unto my said wife, and i do hereby further declare that the expenses of the maintenance and education of my said minor children until they attain the age aforesaid shall be paid and be borne by this my last will.

Sixth: I hereby authorize my said executrix to sell and convey without the intervention or approval of any court, but at her own pleasure the following described portio of the real estate aforesaid mentioned in item first, to wit: the South half of the northwest quarter of the Southeast quarter of Section twenty six (26) in Township thirty (3) Range twenty two (22) in said Green County, and to use the proceeds of such sale for her sole and exclusive use and benefit and in such manner as she may deem proper, and that no court or any person interested in this my said will shall call on her or require her to account for such proceeds of said sale.

Seventh: I further direct that all of my said minor children are to have a home on my homestead farm and with my said wife during their minority.

In witness whereof I have hereunto set my hand this seventh day of April AD 1872.

David C. Murray

Signed and declared by the above named David C. Murry to be his last will and testament in the presence of us who at his request and in his presence have subscribed our names as witnesses thereto,

C.F. Leavitt of Greene Co MO

George Faul   Catharina Bauer of Greene Co Mo   Filed Apr 22nd 1872

David Murray died 9 April, 1872. Inventory of his estate was made by George Faul and H.D. White. It was surprising that his personal property was valued at only $951.50, which included 12 horses, 16 cows, 31 sheep, 30 hogs, 25 cords of wood and some household items. Why were his assets valued so low? In 1870, an average workhorse was selling for $150 and cows were selling at $26 per head. If his animals had been valued at the current market value, his estate would have been over $2000.

Other assets listed were the 320 acres purchased from Tapley Daniel, balance of $2244 on a note from George Kear, a note payable from S.H. Owen for $450 and a note from John and Samuel Austin for $180. There were no accounts listed for notes payable from individuals in Wyandot County and it is doubtful that all the money he had loaned was repaid. It is possible that those accounts were held by Z.G. and not reported in Missouri. Z.G. noted collections on notes payable and sent remittances to David in some of his letters.

David was buried in the Murray Cemetery, located on a hill east of the farmhouse. A receipt was found which said, "Received of H.M. Murray, sixty five dollars payment in full for one set of tombstones from Jas. O'Connell & Co. of St. Louis." David's son, Zelotus ordered a stone for Huldah in 1890, so it is not known if the stones which Huldah ordered were placed in the cemetery. Both stones were similar with clasped hands.

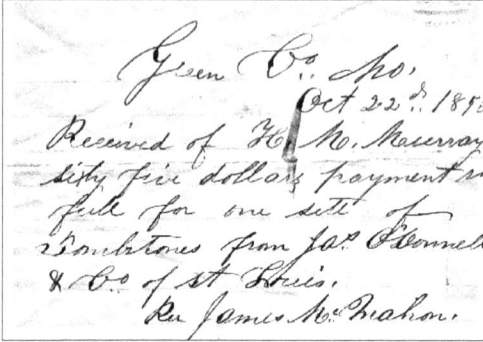

Receipt for David Murray tombstone...

...and the stone.

Family of Rolen and Ezenith Murray Sell

BACK ROW (L to R):	IVA LEE SELL PITTMAN, 1882-....; IRA V. SELL, 1882-1963
SECOND ROW:	ARTHUR SELL, 1870-1912; EDWIN HAMILTON SELL, 1872-1965; WILLIAM WALTER SELL, 1874-1934
THIRD ROW:	CLARA ELDORA SELL McKNIGHT, 1876-1938; ORA MAY SELL WHITE, 1878-....; OLIVE CELESTIA SELL GRISHAM, 1880-1970
FOURTH ROW:	INA LEONA SELL GILLIAM DEGRAFFENREID, 1889-....; JEREMA ANN SELL DIXON, 1886-.... IDA LENORA SELL ACUFF, 1889
FIFTH ROW:	ROLEN CLEMENT SELL, 1849-1941; EZENITH ANN MURRAY SELL, 1852-1922; ANDREW JOHNSON SELL, 1895....

Ezenith Sell and Rolen Sell acknowledged payment of her inheritance on 17 September, 1874. She married Rolen Sell, also of Ohio, on 8 December, 1869. They settled in Polk County, Missouri, and raised twelve children, including two sets of twins.

Isaiah Murray

Isaiah acknowledged receipt of his $100 on 25 October, 1875. Isaiah left home when he was only sixteen, possibly with a member of his mother's family, and went to California. The family story was that he left when Huldah tried to whip him with a black snake whip. His name was found in the California Voter Register 1866-1898 living in Tulare County. He corresponded with his sister Ezenith and she learned that he was killed in a fight shortly after 1875. Z.G. frequently commented on Isaiah in his letters, saying, "We have not heard from Isaiah since spring." Apparently David never saw his son again after Isaiah left home and there were no indications that he corresponded with Isaiah.

Jerema Murray Sterling

There is no record of Jerema Murray Sterling's receipt from her father's estate. She would have received it in Whartonsburg, Ohio, where she and her husband, Hamilton, lived with their two children. Jerema and Hamilton were married 14 August, 1867, shortly before her father and Huldah left for Missouri. They had two children, George and Ethel. Ethel married when she was older and had no children. George and his wife had five children: John J., Herald, Catherine, George, and Lyndis.

Photograph is of Jerema and four of her five grandchildren. She died 20 June, 1911 and is buried with Hamilton, George, and Ethel in McComb Union Cemetery, Hancock County, Ohio. Hamilton died 3 May, 1916.

David's younger children did not receive any money, because according to their father's wishes, they were to remain on the farm and receive property after Huldah's death. Jasper and Zelotus will be covered in Chapter Eight; Andrew J., William and Evaline will be profiled in this section.

Andrew Jackson Murray

Andrew J. Murray and his wife, Lucy Jane.

Andrew Jackson Murray married Lucy Jane Carter on 1 September, 1886. She was the daughter of Hazen Carter and Elizabeth Banfield Carter and the granddaughter of Qualls and Lucy Banfield. This family relationship was probably the reason that Andy was close to his half-brother. See the story of Lawson Banfield in Chapter Seven. After Qualls died, Andy was listed as guardian for Lawson in 1889, but asked the court to relieve him of that obligation in 1890. Lawson maintained contact with the Murray family primarily through Andy. Andy and Lucy's children were Ollie, Edna, Jettie and Carl.

On 20 November, 1886, Andy and Lucy Jane purchased their first piece of land, the first of many properties they bought. Andy was known as a cattle farmer, driving cattle from Arkansas to Greene County and fattening them on his farms. When Andy died in 1934, his estate listed extensive real estate, many loans to individuals, cash on hand and in the bank, and stock certificates in the local stockyards. Total value of his estate was over $132,000, although the appraisers noted that many of the real estate transactions were uncollectable.

Andy died 30 July, 1934. His cause of death was broncho-pneumonia, caused by fractured ribs after being thrown from a horse. He and Lucy Jane were buried at Greenlawn Cemetery, Springfield, Missouri.

William Penn Murray and Family

The youngest son of David and Huldah was William Penn Murray. He married Sarah Jane Stivers, 18 February, 1891. They had a daughter, Maizie, and a son, Norman. A young child named Ralph died when he was only nine months old and was buried in the Murray Cemetery.

William P. Murray died intestate on 20 March, 1911, at the age of forty-three. There were no receipts in his estate file which would indicate health problems and his descendants did not recall a cause of death. Strangely, there is no Missouri Death Certificate, even though Missouri began recording deaths in 1911. He, like his brothers Andy and Zelotus, raised cattle and farmed, owned land, and loaned money to neighbors and relatives. His estate papers show that he was following in the path of his older brothers; however his life was cut short for some unexplained medical reason. William and Janie were buried at Greenlawn Cemetery, Springfield, Missouri.

Evaline Murray Makley

Lena Brune Murray, Marie Makley and Evaline Murray Makley

Evaline, or Evalina, (Evalena) the only daughter of Huldah and David, married John Makley and moved to Dallas, Texas. They had one daughter, Marie. Evaline and John were divorced by the 1910 census because John was not listed in the household and Evaline was employed in Dallas as a stenographer for a book publisher. She died 30 October, 1944, and was buried in the Grove Hill Cemetery, Dallas, Texas.

After David's death, no other letters were found from his brother Z.G. in Ohio. This is surprising because it appeared that the brothers were close and there was no apparent disagreement between them. David trusted Z.G. to handle collections of notes and payments of debts on his behalf. Z.G. wrote that he hoped to visit Missouri and he planned to buy a farm in Greene County until the buyer of his farm in Ohio reneged on the deal. There are indications that Jerema and Hamilton Sterling visited Missouri and reported their visits to Z.G. It is puzzling that there were no further communications found relating to Z.G. or his family.

A visit to Wyandot County led to his grave.

It was startling to find his obituary in the *Wyandot Chief*, 11 July, 1904, describing a horrible accident. It also shows that newspapers liked to tell the lurid and shocking even in those days. There is a one year discrepancy between death dates on his tombstone and the newspaper clipping. Perhaps his stone was placed at a later date and the informant was not certain of the year he died.

MOST HORRIBLE DEATH

Of Squire Z. G. Murray About Noon Saturday at Wharton.

LYING DEAD ON COOK STOVE

With Neck and Breast Awfully Burned and Clothing Afire the Venerable Gentleman is Found by His Horrified Daughter—Was One of Richland Township's Most Honored Pioneers.

A most horrible and fatal accident occurred at Wharton Saturday noon, in the burning to death of Squire Z. G. Murray, one of Richland township's most highly honored pioneers. Since the death of his wife three years ago, he has been living alone. He was in the habit of preparing his own meals although his daughter, Mrs. Peter Cole, who lives near town, came each day to the house and did his housework. About noon Saturday she came to the house, as was her custom, and upon stepping into the kitchen was horrified to see her aged father enveloped in flames and lying on his face upon the top of the cook stove. Mrs. Cole ran to the neighbors at once and informed them of the awful accident which had befallen her father. They returned to the house and upon examination found that he was dead, and his clothing was still burning. The burns upon the unfortunate man are horrible, his beard being burned off, and his neck being burned to a crisp. His clothes down to the waist were entirely consumed in front, the backs of the garments alone remaining upon his body. His breast was also frightfully burned. Dr. J. D. Johnson was called in, but the only assistance he could give was to pronounce Mr. Murray dead.

It is supposed that Squire Murray was working over the stove, preparing his dinner, when he was suddenly seized by a fainting spell or some other ailment and losing consciousness fell face downward upon the stove. The top being red-hot, his clothes became ignited and caused the burns which brought about his death.

Squire Murray was eighty years old and was one of the best known men in this county. He is survived by three children, Wm. Murray, living two miles northeast of Wharton, Mrs. A. C. Ward, also living northeast of Wharton, and Mrs. Peter Cole, who lives north of Wharton.

The funeral of Squire Z. G. Murray was held from the Methodist church at Wharton, Sunday afternoon, at 2:30 o'clock, Rev. R. Wright conducted the services. Burial was made in the cemetery at Wharton.

Letters written from Z.G. to David may be accessed at the Special Collections and Archives, Missouri State University, Springfield, Missouri.

Bibliography

(1) DeMuth, I. MacDonald. *History of Pettus County, Missouri.* F.A. North: 1882

(2) White, Helen Murray. *Butterfield Overland Mail Route, a History of Early Settlers along Boonville Road in Northern Greene County.* Heritage Books: Berwyn Heights. Md. 2014.

Photograph of Huldah Murray, date unknown.

7

Huldah Murray

Huldah Murray was only thirty-three when she became a widow and assumed responsibility for her family and the homestead. A neighbor, Qualls Banfield, was recently widowed and the two decided to marry. Were there no hard feelings between Banfield and the wife of David Murray after the Tapley Daniel lawsuit? Apparently not. Perhaps Huldah felt comfortable marrying a neighbor who was well-known to her husband.

However, Huldah was a smart woman and she required an ante-nuptial agreement before she married Qualls. No doubt she wanted to protect the financial interests of her children. Their agreement was signed 29 November, 1873, and they were married 30 November, 1873.

Terms of the agreement were: (1) Huldah agreed to place all her personal property in the house to be occupied by both parties; she also agreed to place her livestock and farming utensils with the party of the second part. (2) The title to one undivided half of all personal property, livestock and farming implements would remain Huldah's property and used for her personal benefit and that property should in no way be used to pay for the debts of Banfield. (3) In case of death or dissolution of the marriage, she would be entitled to all her household property and one half of the properties acquired during the marriage. (4) In case of death, the properties of each party would go to the heirs of the party. (5) Huldah would have the right to go to court in her own name or in the name of her best friend.

In reviewing the ante-nuptial agreement, it seems surprising that she would agree to place her livestock and farming utensils with her new husband. How would her sons maintain the homestead without livestock for income? It is possible that the personal property owned by David may have already been divided between Huldah and her sons; that is not clear in the agreement.

In 1875, Huldah and Qualls had a son, Roger Lawson. In May 1877, they were divorced, the divorce awarded to petitioner, Banfield. Her married name (Murray) was restored and she was permitted to marry again.

Strangely enough, in February 1879, Huldah and Qualls re-married. Five months later, on 5 July, 1879, Huldah Murray died, cause unknown. She was buried beside her first husband, David Murray in the Murray Cemetery. Qualls Banfield declined to serve as executor of her estate and T.S. Wilson, a neighbor, was appointed executor. Qualls may have declined, because according to family stories, Huldah's sons were not happy about their marriage.

A receipt was found dated 7 July, 1879, from Doling & Langenberg, for fifteen yards alpaca, one black lace tie, one pair black kid gloves, one pair ladies white hose, one pair of slippers for a cost of $10.65. This gives a description of Huldah's burial clothes. Where was the viewing, at the Murray house or the Banfield house?

Huldah's estate was appraised by neighbors, Alexander Evans, William Fulbright, and Hosea Mullings. One collectible asset in the appraisal inventory was $12.50 due from Aaron Glidewell for the sale of an old house. Was this the Daniel house where David and Huldah lived with their children?

Personal property listed indicated that her house was fully furnished. Huldah's children, Zelotus, Jasper, Andrew, William and Evaline each received a bedstead. Little Roger received a trundle bed. A bureau, table, chairs, rocking chairs, dining room set, stove, tableware, spinning wheel and a sewing machine were divided between the children. Horses, cows and hogs were given to the six children for a total value of $142 inheritance for each of them. Since none of the heirs were married, the Murray children remained on the homestead and Roger remained with his father. No value was assigned to the real estate; apparently it was understood that the land would be divided equally between the children, as David had indicated in his will.

Following is an example of how the assets were divided between the children.

There was one difference between David's estate and Huldah's estate. The family no longer lived in the frame house left by the Daniel family, because in 1877, Huldah started building the house she wanted, similar to the house she left in Ohio. One wonders why the house was not built earlier—or while David was still alive.

It may have been due to the Panic of 1873, which began shortly after David died. The Panics of 1837 and 1857 were linked to defaults of railroad investments, and those factors occurred again in 1873. It began with the crash of the Vienna stock market and rippled across Europe, finally hitting major banks in the United States with the fall of the Jay Cooke & Co. The Cooke Company was heavily invested in railroads and when it suddenly announced that it would suspend withdrawals, there was wide-spread panic followed by bank failures, commercial bankruptcies and unemployment. The New York Stock Exchange closed for ten days. This was known at the time as the Long Depression, lasting into the 1890s. Perhaps this was the reason that Huldah did not begin her house until 1877.

In October 1877, Huldah bought wood, shingles, flooring, lath, windows, doors and paint from S.W. McLaughlin, proprietor of Springfield Planing Mill, located at the corner of Phelps Avenue and Campbell Street. The final bill from McLaughlin on 1 November, 1878, was for $377.

The Pictorial and Genealogical Record of Greene County, contained high praise for the mill, saying: "The Springfield Planing Mill and Lumber Company has been one of the most prominent in its line of work, and as all the machinery in use is of the latest improved and most costly kind, it has always been found equal to the demands placed on it." (1)

Springfield, Mo. Sept 12 1878

Mrs H. M. Murray

Bought of **S. W. McLAUGHLIN,**

PROPRIETOR OF SPRINGFIELD PLANING MILL,

And Dealer in Lumber, Lath, Sash, Doors, Blinds, Shingles, &c.

CORNER PHELPS AVENUE AND CAMPBELL STREET.

	1877					
Dct	8	366 ft 2 inch Dressed	at	30	10 98	
		109 " 1 3/4 " "	"	50	5 44	
	12	58 " 2 inch "		30	1 74	
	23	1/2 Gal paint			1 10	
1878	24	27 " 2/10 16 ft		2 1/2	66	19 86
Mar	20	164 " 4 in Molding		4c	6 56	
		140 " 2h "		2 50	3 50	
		320 " of Stops		75c	2 40	
		376 " Common Bds		25	9 40	21 86
"	26	10 M Shingles	at	4 50	40 00	40 00
	26	6 Windows 12/18	"	2 30	13 80	
		7 " 12/14	"	1 80	12 60	
		4 M Shingles	"	4 00	16 00	42 40
"	11	Galns paint		1 90	7 60	7 60
"	13	990 ft of flooring		3 00	29 70	
		240 " " YP flg		3 00	7 20	36 90
May	23	210 " " A Stock		4 50	9 45	9 45
June	1	82 " " 1 3/4 1 1/2 inch		5 00	4 11	
		62 " " YP		3 00	1 86	
		5 Doors 2/8 1 3/4 "		1 85	9 25	
		2 " 2/6 "		1 20	2 40	
		1 " 2/6 " 1 1/2		1 70	1 70	19 35
"		2 M " Lath		4 50	8 00	
		602 ft of flooring		2 75	16 55	24 55
Sept	8	328 " " W P 1 inch		3 50	11 45	
		144 " " flooring		2 50	3 60	
		400 " " 1/4 Round		75c	3 00	
		32 " " 5/8 pannell		4 00	1 28	19 36
	11	56 " " Selects		3 25	1 82	
		32 " " 4 inch Molding		3 50	1 12	
		32 " " 2/4		2 25	72	3 66
	11	2 1/2 M " Lath		3 75	9 38	
		43 ft of 2/4 8		2 25	97	
		98 " " 1/4 Round		75	75	
		over			1 10	$244.99

There were also individual receipts for wagonloads of brick, which, according to family stories, were hauled by her sons, one wagonload at a time. The receipts totaled at least 26,301 bricks. On the following page, there are samples of the tickets for each load of bricks, beginning in August 1877.

They were purchased from Wesson Brick Yard, located on Grant Street, north of Central Street in Springfield. William Wesson was listed in the *Springfield*

City Directory 1873-74 at that address. He owned five tracts of land along Grant Street. William died in 1876 and his widow Narcissa operated the brick yard until her son, M.B., took over the operation. M.B. Wesson was listed as proprietor of Wesson Brick Yard in the *History & Directory of Springfield and North Springfield*. The address was 705 N. Grant. In probate records for William Wesson, there were bills from the Springfield Planing Mill; apparently the two businesses worked together.

Brick for Mrs Murray.	
No of Tickets	No of Bricks
Ticket .. 58	800
61	500
62	406
63	500
64	500
65	300
66	600
67	500
68	518
69	500
70	500
71	500
72	500
73	400
74	264
75	426
76	400
77	400
78	500
79	500
80	400
81	1300
82	400
83	500
84	566
85	800
86	365
87	485
88	517
89	400
90	520
91	600
92	1000
93	400
94	200
95	500
96	440
97	500

Receipts for loads of bricks.

FRONT ELEVATION.

The house was an Italianate style, popular in the mid-1800s. House plans published in the *Canada Farmer Magazine*, April 1865, look much like the house that Huldah built. Chief features of the Italianate farmhouse were: Low pitched or flat roof, balanced symmetrical shape, two or three stories, overhanging eaves or cornices, a cupola, tall, narrow double paned windows and arches above windows and doors.

The house plan described in the magazine article had dimensions of 28 x 42 feet and the author had these suggestions: "It is the common practice of some of our farmers to take all their meals in the kitchen; this is a habit which marks a low state of society. Our agricultural population should not scorn comfort and refinement. Every grace that belongs to rural life should be found amongst the daughters of our farmers." He then suggested that the bedrooms should be well-ventilated, large and airy.

Huldah's house was 30 x 30 feet and lacked some of the decorative features; however the square shape, cupola, placement of fireplaces, windows and front door bear a similarity. This is the first photograph available showing a comparison between the farmhouse in the *Canada Farmer* and the house which Huldah built.

This photo was probably taken about 1894, because Walter was born in 1893. Z.G. is pictured with his wife Lena and his children from his first marriage to Maggie. Left to right are: Susan, Evaline, Walter, Z.G., Luther, Lena. Jasper is leaning on the gate. Z.G. is wearing his black stockman's hat.

There were no receipts found which would indicate who built the house. It is doubtful that Huldah's sons were skilled enough to construct the house, although they could have worked on it with proper guidance. There is no record of where the foundation stones were found. Were they purchased? Probably not. They closely resemble some of the large limestone rocks found on the property.

It is a mystery why Huldah completed this house in 1878 and re-married Qualls Banfield in February, 1879. Did she live with Qualls and leave her children on the home place? It is doubtful that Qualls left his home and lived with her. After the original divorce, the annulment agreement would have been void and her household goods would have been placed in the brick house. This is another unanswered puzzle.

After Huldah's death, the 1880 census of Robberson Township, Greene County, Missouri, named Jasper Murray age 22, as head of the household. Other members were Zelotus age 19, Andrew age 14, William age 12, and Evaline age 9. Also living in the house was Fred Hofman, listed as farm laborer.

His wife's occupation was keeping house for the family. With Fred Hofman, his wife and their three children, plus the five Murray children, the house was full of people. There were four bedrooms upstairs in the Murray house; perhaps one or two of the rooms downstairs were converted to bedrooms.

Two receipts were found relating to Evaline. "Received of T.S. Wilson, Curator of Evalina Murray, this 28th day of August 1880, eighty cents for cutting and making two dresses for the said Evalina Murray." Signed by Mrs. Hoffman. The second receipt was to Mrs. D. J. Kirkpatrick for three months school tuition at $1.50, commencing in March and ending in June, 1880. One wonders in which household this young girl lived as her mother moved back and forth between the Murray house and the Banfield house.

Roger, the son of Huldah and Qualls was living with his father in the 1880 census. The census report listed Roger Banfield (Qualls), his wife Alice, a step-son James, Roger age 5, and Fanny Banfield. The age listed for Roger (the son) is important because on later documents, Roger gave different dates for his birth.

On 5 November, 1879, Qualls married Mrs. Aulsie (Alice) McGrew. The step-son must have been Aulsie's son by a prior marriage. Fanny Banfield was a black family servant, believed to have come from Tennessee with the Warren family, the family of Qualls' first wife. Qualls, Lucy Warren Banfield and Fanny Banfield were all buried in the Banfield cemetery on the Banfield farm. The Banfield farm is now owned by the Springfield-Greene County Park Board and is called Lost Hill Park.

Qualls Banfield died in 1887 and there are no family stories to indicate where Roger Lawson lived after that. He may have lived with his half-brother Andrew Jackson and his wife, because A.J. kept in contact with Roger after he left Greene County. See more information on Roger Lawson in Chapter Nine.

Bibliography:
(1) *Pictorial and Genealogical Record of Greene County, Missouri.* Chicago: Goodspeed Brothers, 1893.

8

The Older Children — Jasper and Zelotus

After Huldah's death, Jasper and Zelotus probably farmed the land together. There are a few receipts to show their common actions, but there are no family stories to help solve the puzzles which occurred between 1880 and 1883.

Jasper and Z.G. purchased fire insurance on Huldah's house from the German Insurance Company of Freeport, Illinois. They insured the house for $400 value at a cost of $8 for five years dated 18 December, 1880.

In 1880, Z.G. was a young man of nineteen, and his first documented action was to borrow $95 on September 20th from Martin Polson of Bolivar, Missouri. In the 1880 census, Polson's occupation was listed as "freighting," leading one to wonder what Z.G. was having transported, and to what location? The terms were payment of $95 in ten days with "interest from maturity at the rate of ten percent per annum." Martin Polson is not known in family history, nor is the reason for this loan.

For the year 1880, Z.G. was taxed 94 cents for personal property and Jasper was taxed $1.96 for personal property. Both tax bills were paid 18 December, 1880. The boys received the same disbursement from their mother's estate—did Z.G. dispose of some of his personal property in 1880? Why did Jasper have a higher assessed personal property valuation than his brother?

Was there a dispute between Jasper and Zelotus in 1881 or 1882? Did they disagree over farming practices or ownership of personal property? Or did Jasper decide that he did not want the responsibility of farm ownership and raising the younger children? It seems unusual that the oldest son would not want to buy out his siblings and own the land; however, he may have not had money for that choice. It doesn't seem that there was any urgency to break up the real estate.

Sometime after the 1880 census when Jasper was listed as head of the household and before November 1881, Jasper Murray was married to Maggie LNU, as evidenced by her appearance before a Greene County notary on 3 November, 1881, to be examined as the wife of Jasper Murray.

On 3 December, 1881, Jasper and Maggie Murray executed a quit claim deed for Jasper's part of the Murray farm. Z.G. paid $200 to Jasper, with a promissory note to pay the balance of $600 in increments of $200 per year with six percent interest. A condition of the deed of trust was that it could not be foreclosed until all three notes were due, as was agreed between the parties.

Photograph of Jasper Murray, date unknown.

Who was Maggie LNU, the wife of Jasper? There was no marriage record for her and Jasper in Greene or Polk Counties. It was not uncommon for local ministers to marry a couple and fail to register those marriages with local authorities. It is possible that happened in this case.

A receipt found in the Murray papers could give a clue about Maggie, but it raises more questions than answers. Maggie Gay was awarded a divorce from William Gay on 16 November, 1881, after the defendant "refused to obey any of the obligations imposed on him by his marital obligations and treated her with contempt and refused to live with & support Ptft." Henry Fleckenstein paid $4.10 for the plaintiff as full settlement in the case, receipt dated 19 November, 1881.

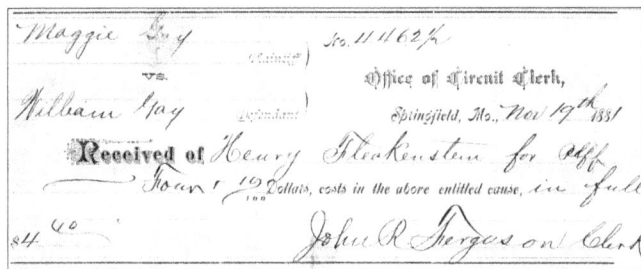

In the 1870 census, Joshua Gay, with a son William, was living next to the family of Solomon Owen, a neighbor to the Murray family. William was still living with his father's family in the 1880 census. He was listed as age twenty-three years, single. No marriage record has been found for William Gay and Maggie LNU in either Greene or Polk Counties. If they were married, it must have been for a very short time. The date of this payment and the date of the quit claim deed are so close that one would believe Maggie Gay married Jasper Murray. Is there any other reason that the divorce receipt would be in the Murray papers?

There is another puzzling aspect to this story. Henry Fleckenstein, who paid the $4.10 for Maggie Gay, was not a lawyer. He was the son-in-law of Jacob Rosenberger, living in the Rosenberger household in the 1880 census. Jacob's daughter, Maggie, married Z.G. Murray in 1883. What was Maggie Gay's relationship to the Rosenberger family? Did Z.G. meet Maggie Rosenberger through Maggie Gay and Jasper Murray? Or, would it be a far-fetched question to wonder if Maggie Gay was the same person as Maggie Rosenberger? These questions, like so many others in family histories, leave one puzzled and curious, and unfortunately disappointed that the answers will not be found.

Family stories said that Jasper "sold out" and left the country. He returned a few years later minus his wife. When asked about her, he reportedly said, "I don't know that's any of your business." He must have stayed in Greene County until April because he paid personal property taxes on 15 April, 1882, and returned in October, 1885. He wasn't out of the county very long.

After Jasper sold his interest in the farm, he never owned property again. His lifestyle was completely different from his brothers, his father and his ancestors in Ohio and New York, who owned land, loaned money, and became leaders in the community.

Jasper spent his remaining years working as a day laborer for his brothers, nephews or neighbors. He lived with one family and then abruptly moved on to live with another relative. When he was not working, he was reading his Bible. He may have been a lover of history, maybe politics. In old books found at the Murray home, his name was written in the front of a book, *"The Lost Cause, A New Southern History of the War of the Confederates,"* published 1866. Jasper never re-married, died in 1940, and was buried in Greenlawn Cemetery, Springfield, Missouri. He lived longer than his brothers.

After Jasper sold his interest in the farm, Zelotus (Z.G. or Lotz) married Maggie Rosenberger on 20 December, 1883. The ceremony was performed by Rev. Kirk Baxter and recorded in Greene County marriages on 24 December, 1883. Maggie and Z.G.'s oldest child, Susan, was born 5 January, 1883, eleven months before their marriage. The discrepancy between their marriage date and Susan's birthdate could indicate that Maggie and Z.G. had a relationship before their marriage. Where did Maggie live before she married Z.G.? Did she live on the farm and help care for the younger siblings, or did she live with her parents?

Or, did this happen: Susan was conceived in April 1882, and Jasper paid his personal property tax in April 1882. This was the last documented date that indicated he was in Greene County until he returned in 1885. Did Jasper abandon Maggie because he did not want the responsibility of fatherhood?

In May 1885, Z.G. sought for a partition of the real estate of David Murray. The minor heirs, Andrew Jackson, William, Evalina Murray and Lawson Banfield, were defendants in the case. On 16 October, 1885, Jasper appeared before a notary and acknowledged that he signed the quit claim deed. Maggie did not appear.

One thing is certain. Z.G. could not have bought the real estate without the financial help of his father-in-law. The Greene County Circuit Court ordered the sheriff of Greene County to sell the real estate at public auction on the court house steps. On 14 November, 1885, the sale was held and the highest bidders were Zelotus G. Murray and Jacob Rosenberger. This sale transferred the Murray property to Zelotus and his heirs. Years later, there were disgruntled comments from the younger siblings about this sale, but because of their minor status in 1885, they had no opportunity to object.

The abstract of the Murray farm had an entry stating that on 10 February, 1885, Z.G. Murray wrote a promissory note to his father-in-law, Jacob Rosenberger, promising to pay $700 within three years at six percent interest.

Papers in the Z.G. Murray file show the original note, with the signature torn out, a common way of showing that the loan had been paid.

In addition to paying this note, Z.G. had to pay pasture rent to Andrew, William and Evalina, as evidenced by receipts in his papers. It is not clear whether he paid rent to Lawson Banfield.

Zelotus' payments to his siblings.

When Jacob Rosenberger's will was filed in 1892, his assets listed a loan of $3,000 to Z.G. Murray. In Z.G.'s papers, a note was found which was made on 8 January, 1891 for $3,000 payable on or before 1 March, 1898, at six percent interest. The signature was torn out, indicating that the note was paid.

The years between 1883 and 1891 were filled with hard work and sadness for the family of Z.G. and Maggie. They had three children who lived to adulthood: Susan, born 5 January, 1883; Evaline, born 6 January, 1885; and Luther Jacob, born 4 January, 1889. Maggie must have had a difficult life with children born every two years and the tragedy of their son, Freddie, who was born 29 June, 1887 and died 21 December, 1887. Family members said that one of the children was holding Freddie when he fell into the fireplace and was severely burned, which resulted in his death. What a heartbreaking Christmas for the family. An unnamed baby died shortly after Maggie's death on 29 July, 1891. Maggie, Freddie and the infant were buried in the Murray family cemetery.

A receipt from Ely Paxon, Undertaker and Embalmer, was found dated 10 August, 1891. It was for a case box and shroud, total $25.50, an expense for Maggie's death and burial.

Ely Paxon came to Missouri in 1868 from Findley, Ohio. He learned cabinet making and undertaking in Ohio and went to work for Julius Kassler when he moved to Springfield. Paxon went into partnership with Kassler and later owned his own company. He was one of the undertakers who were well known and respected in Springfield.

Perhaps after Freddie's death, Maggie wanted the family cemetery cleaned and maintained. A receipt was found dated 6 February, 1888, showing expenses for fencing, a post, and lumber for the gate. On 10 February, an itemized receipt showed names of the workers: Z.G. Murray, two day's work; Andy Murray, two day's work; William Murray, two day's work; William Jones, two day's work; Lewis H. Dickens, two day's work; James Dickens one and one-half day's work. William Jones, Lewis Dickens and James Dickens were later buried in the cemetery. A man named Burleson worked six and one-half days. With all these men working, it appears that the cemetery must have been a jungle. Jasper Murray was not one of the workers, although he was living in Greene County.

In February 1890, Z.G. bought tombstones from Buffalo Marble Works. One was of Italian marble, three and one-half feet high, with clasped hands and a bead to be full round and to run to within thirteen inches of bottom of the slab. The stone was for Huldah M. Murray, wife of David C. Murray. There was no purchase for David Murray's stone. Perhaps the earlier stone purchased by Huldah had already been placed there.

The second stone purchased was for a white marble stone, with a lamb carved on top, and the words engraved, "Here rests in God our beloved son." Also engraved was the inscription, "Freddie, son of Z.G. and Maggie Murray."

The orders were signed, "Z.G.Murray, his mark X." On the 1910 census, the census taker had marked that Z.G. could read, but not write and all of his legal documents were signed with "X." It seems strange that he did not learn to write because his brothers signed their names, and they did not use an "X." It is not known if he had a learning disability or that he didn't have early education because he was only six years old when his parents came to Missouri.

It is interesting to compare real estate tax receipts from 1882, 1883, and 1887. In 1882, Jasper and Z.G. were shown as owners of the farm. In 1883, only Z.G. was listed because Jasper had sold his interest and in 1887, Z.G. and his father-in-law were owners. The receipts confirm land ownership for those years. However by 1887 the real estate taxes were less than in 1882. Greene County taxes and school taxes were reduced.

Also revealing are the 1890 Greene County Missouri personal property tax records. William and Z.G. were beginning to accumulate their farm property. They were assessed taxes for the following personal property:

William P. Murray: 2 horses, 1 mule, 4 cattle, 20 sheep, 7 hogs, $700 money, $21 other personal property. Tax, $9.77.

Z.G. Murray: 4 horses, 2 mules, 32 cattle, 9 hogs, $100 money. Tax, $7.42.

Jasper and Andrew Murray were not listed in these tax records.

9

Zelotus Murray's Family

International events of the 1890s such as the Spanish-American War and the Yukon Gold Rush probably caused no reaction among Murray family members. Closer events such as the invasion of the boll weevil in Texas and the devastation of the cotton crop, as well as finding oil in Texas, might have had more relevance. Locally, the progress of railroads and incorporation of many local businesses catering to an agricultural economy would be of greater interest to farmers. All of these events were covered in local newspapers, which would have been read by members of the Murray family.

After Maggie died, Z.G. needed a wife to help care for his young children. How did he meet Lena C. Brune? Did he associate with German families who were settling in Springfield in the late 1800s? Did he meet Lena through the Rosenberger family or their neighbors? There were no family stories to answer these questions.

Lena C. Brune

On 20 January, 1892, Z.G. married Lena C. Brune. She was the daughter of Louis and Wilhelmina Brune, who immigrated to the United States in 1873. Louis and Wilhelmina possibly left the village of Bartolfelde, Germany, because Louis was the younger son in his family and could not inherit family property. Lena and her sister Minnie were born in Germany. Her brother Louis was born in Ohio and her brother Henry and sister Racie were born in Missouri.

Lena and Z.G. had three children of their own: Walter Henry, born 1893; Dorsey Louis, born 1896; Mamie Wilhelmina Huldah, born 1898.

The following picture shows the oldest son Luther, Z.G. and his three youngest children. It looks as if Lena had a hand in decorating the house and insisting on a new front porch.

There were numerous receipts in Z.G.'s papers for machinery purchases, items which a prosperous farmer would need. In 1886 he purchased a light elevator binder, five foot ext. from Aultman, Miller and Co. It was paid off in 1887 at eight percent interest. In 1887 he purchased a Springfield Wagon. A receipt was found dated 24 April, 1887, for payment of $46.25, with promise to pay the balance at ten percent interest.

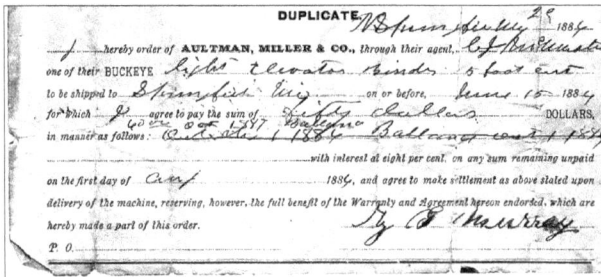

Lena seldom socialized with neighbors, but a letter was found from a neighbor or relative inviting Lena and her family to a supper at Glidewell Church. A fundraiser for church pews was planned and the letter indicated what kind of food women would bring. Note the meat, bread and pies and absence of vegetables. (Of course in December there were few vegetables available except what might have been canned or kept in the cellar.) The Elex (Alex) Evans and wife referred to in the letter are descendants of Joseph Evans who operated the Evans' Station, the last stop on the Butterfield Overland Mail Route before the stage stopped in Springfield. (See *Butterfield Overland Mail-Early Settlers in Northern Greene County*.)

Receipts were found for drugs, clothing and food from merchants in Springfield. The receipts from Commercial Street businesses authenticate when and where they were located. After the railroad was built to Springfield, Commercial Street became a thriving location for businesses catering to agriculture and transportation.

Perhaps as a symptom of Z.G.'s success and desire to enter the modern era, on 9 December, 1903, he purchased an interest in the Springfield and Robberson Prairie Telephone Company. For $33.50, the family owned their own telephone!

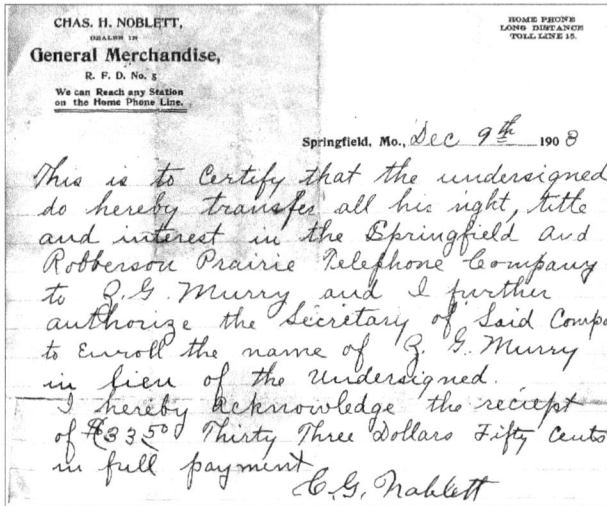

At right is a photo of the front page of the 1904 directory. The directory stated that it contained the names of 1,975 subscribers, commercial and residential, "a gain of 400 since May."

Inside information containing names, addresses and phone numbers has been photocopied and is located at the Greene County Archives, Springfield, Missouri.

Mullings School, ca. 1908.

The Murray children and their neighbors attended school at the Mullings School, which later became known as Glidewell School. It was common for students to graduate from eighth grade with their education complete. Some of the students in this photo look too old to be in the eighth grade, but their attendance was interrupted due to farm work, harvests and sometimes illnesses.

Above is a picture of children enrolled at Mullings School. The photo was taken ca. 1908 and some of the children have been identified. Walter, Dorsey and Mamie are in the picture, as are Andy's children, Carl and Jettie. Note that standing next to Walter is Robbie Fallin, whom he later married.

At left, the picture shows Andy J. and Z.G. with their horses. Note the black stockman hat which Z.G. was wearing. Apparently he was rarely without that hat.

In 1904 the World's Fair opened in St. Louis. It was the largest in history and commemorated the one hundred years since the Louisiana Purchase and the progress made in industry and agriculture. The site chosen was over 1200 acres and contained more than 1500 buildings. In addition, the United States celebrated its entry into international affairs by having a mile-long Pike, lined with cafes and restaurants, where visitors could dine on strange new dishes served at the Chinese Village, the Streets of Cairo, the Irish Village and the Tyrolean Restaurant.

Sometime during that year, Z.G. and Andy J. boarded the train in Springfield and left for the World's Fair. It is possible that Andy's wife, Janie, may have accompanied them, but Lena did not. She was always afraid of crowds and did not socialize with many people. Z.G. bought souvenirs for the children—little purses with the inscription, "World's Fair St. Louis 1904."

No doubt Z.G. and Andy enjoyed the exhibits at the Palace of Agriculture. Products of farms from around the United States were on display, as well as products from Central and South America. Florida had a hybridized version of the pomelo. Pomelos sold for the price of five dollars a box, and were later known as grapefruit. Perhaps Z.G. tasted a hot dog, iced tea, cotton candy, and an ice cream cone. There were no records from the trip, only the souvenir purses.

In the society section of the *Springfield Republican*, June 1904, individuals were named who were either going to or had just returned from the World's Fair. Most of them went to St. Louis on the Frisco Railway. A special price was advertised for "Missouri Day," scheduled for June 3.

Hotel prices were probably most expensive inside the grounds. The advertisement on the next page is for rooms at the Inside Inn, located inside the fair grounds.

FIRST AID TO THE FATIGUED.

Home at The Inside Inn Inside the
Fair Grounds Insures Pleasant
Visit to the World's Fair.

No Extortion Here—The Rates Are
Fixed by the Authorities.

So much is there to be seen at the
World's Fair that one might start at
the beginning, eat and sleep on the
way and still not see everything were
a month's time consumed in the tour
of exposition streets and aisles.

Frail humanity would not be equal
to such a task, but there has been
a way provided by which the visit
may see the exposition in its fullness
and to the best advantage with as little loss of time and energy as possible.

The Inside Inn is situated on the
exposition grounds, where the visitor
who wishes to spend his time pro-
fitably may secure accommodations
that will enable him to arise with the
awakening of the exposition, just outside his windows, and begin a tour of
inspection that can continue until
long after the mantle of night spreads
over the spectacle. Then a refuge will
be afforded him right at hand.

No struggle with the crowds, wait-
ing for street cars or pushing a way
to the ticket booths for guests of the
Inside Inn. All of these discomforts
have been saved him by an arrange-
ment with the exposition by which he
may stay inside the grounds as long
as he is a guest at the hotel. He will
have not only the comforts of the
spacious hotel, on one of the coolest
and most beautiful spots of the exposition, but the privilege of the par-
lors, reception rooms, offices and ver-
andas, where he may rest at interval's
during the day and mingle with agreeable company.

The Inside Inn is on the intramural
railway, which penetrates every part
of the grounds, and it is near the
Plateau of States, overlooking the
main picture of the fair. It is reached
from Union station by three car lines.
The Inside Inn has 1000 rooms at $1.50
per person; 500 at $2.00 and 500 at
$2.50. The total number of rooms is
2,257.

Prices were $1.50, $2.00 or $2.50 per person per night. However, there was an advertisement published in another section of the paper for rooms at $1 per night, located outside the grounds, with trolley cars running to the fairgrounds.

There were letters from family members asking about Z.G.'s health, expressing concern and commenting about him being in the hospital. In pictures when he was a young man, he appeared stout and somewhat overweight. However in a photo with Lena, his obesity was obvious.

He must have been concerned about his weight problem because an advertisement and letter were found from F.J. Kellogg, Battle Creek, Michigan. Mr. Kellogg advertised that his pills turned fat into muscle. He offered to cut the price of an order from $10 to a special price of $3.33.

REDUCES WEIGHT
WITHOUT DANGER

TURNS FAT
INTO MUSCLE

F. J. KELLOGG

RATIONAL TREATMENT FOR OBESITY

"MAKES FAT PEOPLE LEAN"

July 27/06

KELLOGG BUILDING
BATTLE CREEK, MICH.

Z. G. Murray,
Springfield, Mo.

My dear Sir:

When you wrote me for my free trial package of Obesity Food Tablets some time ago, I took it for granted, of course, that you were suffering from excess fat, for mere curiosity could hardly prompt one to write on such a matter as this. Now I am frank to say that I cannot understand what is holding you back in placing your order for a full month's treatment when so much depends on it. Not only are you annoyed and distressed by this unfortunate condition, but your appearance your usefulness, your peace of mind, your energy, your activity and you safety all suffer by reason of it. I cannot believe that you are skeptical of my ability to cure you after you have read such convincing and conclusive proof in the hundreds of unsolicited testimonial letters I have sent you. If there is any such thing as absolute proof by means of the testimony of others, I have certainly proved to you that these Obesity Food Tablets will cure you, beyond the remote possibility of a doubt.

Now, I can only think of one reason that may be standing in your way and that is the question of price. It may be that you do not find it convenient to spare $10.00, the regular price, for a full month's treatment. Now I am going to make you a very unusual offer and one that I have never made before, and I do it for two reasons. One is that I want to help all who answer my advertisements and know that I can do it if I have the opportunity. Another and more selfish reason is that I want to get my Obesity Food introduced into every community in the land so that it will be heard of and known by every man, woman and child suffering from excess fat. I know that a benefitted and satisfied patient is the very best possible advertisement I can have, and I know that after you shall have received the great benefits of this wonderful Obesity Food and been completely cured of your unfortunate trouble, you will not hesitate to speak out and let it be known and tell your friends and acquaintances of its great merit.

With this in view, I propose to send you the full month's treatment, the regular price of which is $10.00, for just what it costs me to prepare it, put it up and send it to you, including of course, office expenses necessary to carry on a business. I shall not make one cent on it. I will send you the full month's treatment on receipt of $3.93 which just lets me out of the proposition. I do this, as I said before, for the benefit of your advertisement, for I find on looking over my books that I have not sent the Obesity Food Treatment to any one in your immediate neighborhood. This is an experiment with me, but I am going to try it and see how it works out, and meanwhile you are getting the benefit of it. Remember that this is a confidential matter and you are not to say a word to any one else about the price I have made

An entry on Find A Grave, Ancestry.com, provided a little insight into F.J. Kellogg and his pills. Although his address was Battle Creek, Michigan, he was not related to the famous Kellogg cereal family. According to the website, F.J. Kellogg became a millionaire as the manufacturer and promoter of Professor Kellogg's Brown Tablets, although he used the name Obesity Food Tablets when corresponding with Z.G. According to the post, Kellogg's patent medicines were among the first investigated by the precursor to the FDA. The active ingredient in the Obesity Food Tablets was found to be poke (*Phytolacca Americana*), a traditional Indian folk remedy for weight loss, highly toxic. Ingesting smaller amounts during a meal might cause diarrhea. If Lena had known the ingredient, she could have picked enough poke growing around the fields; however, poke can only be eaten in early spring. It is toxic after berries form on the plant. It's good to know that Z.G. did not spend his money on these worthless pills.

On 19 April, 1906, Jerema wrote to her brother. She said she was getting old. "I was 57 the 8th if this month." She refers to her husband Ham (Hamilton Sterling) and her son George and daughter Ethel. She also mentioned trouble in Springfield. One wonders how quickly news traveled. On April 16, three young black men were killed by a lynch mob on the public square.

On 26 January, 1910, Jerema wrote again that Ezenith had written to her that Zelotus was sick and was going to the hospital. She expressed her wish that they could see each other. The "Masy" she was referring to would be William and Jennie's daughter, indicating that she corresponded with William's family.

In December 1909, Z.G. received a letter from his Aunt Moll. She was the younger sister of his mother, Huldah. Her name was Mary Ellen Doud and she married John Baker.

Her letter is ten pages long and the information contained in the letter gives insights into family relationships. Aunt Moll talked about her family and described her Christmas decorations and presents for the family. She wrote lovingly about Huldah's descendants and expressed concern about Z.G.'s health, saying that Andy had written to her. She instructed her nephew to "give your heart to Jesus. He can help and he can save."

Notes on Aunt Moll's letter
Page 3: These relatives are on her husband's side of the family. She refers to "Hendricks was married just before we left last fall," and another son who went with the same woman "when we was there last fall." This indicates that she visited the family in Missouri in 1908 or 1909.

Page 4: On this page Aunt Moll refers to Allie Banfield, Roger Lawson Banfield's wife and to Marie Makely, daughter of Evaline Murray Makely.

1.

You can save money six days out of the week by trading at
THE WAUGH SHOE STORE.
31 Public Square, LIMA, OHIO.

Dec the 8 1909.

Harrod Ohio

My dear Nephew Lotie as I love to call you.
I This evening got 3 letters & one was from Andy, saying you was sick. Now John & I sympathise with you. Get the best medical aid you can you are young & have a good chance to get well. Lena will wait on you good. Remember to keep in good heart & try & think you will get well will help you along much I know from experience. Now Lotie we would come & see you if it was

2.

not so far, but rest assured that we love my dear sisters boy & family. Lotie cant you give your heart to Jesus. he can help & he can save. Think of the many blessinge we have from day to day. I feel that I have been blessed after so much sickness as I have had can say I am well for my age. John is well. One of the letters was from Naaman. he has been sick for one week with Rheumatism. Hendricks the one that

3.

You can save money six days out of the week by trading at
THE WAUGH SHOE STORE.
31 Public Square, LIMA, OHIO.

3rd

was married just before we left last fall. They have a baby boy a very weakly babe call him Hendrick Maurice. L C is still at home & goes with the same one that he went with when we was there Blanche Morry.
Altha & Will has bought a property in Harrod not far from us, she helps me with the work & is so much comfort to me. Bertsil still lives in Saphire. & them Naaman was all home last summer.

4.

4th

You can save money six days out of the week by trading at
THE WAUGH SHOE STORE.
31 Public Square, LIMA, OHIO.

We are having very cold blustery weather, have a new hard coal base burner, & do not like it very well, but I guess when we learn to use it we will like it better. I got a letter from Allie Banfield & a card from Marie makly latly both familys well. I suppose you knew Evalina & John was divorced.
Hurry up & get well Lotie & you & Lena come out to our place so as to be here on Xmas, we

5.

5th to have a good dinner
as a Xmas comes in the
Parlor. The children & a few
of the kin folks will be here
& instead of a xmas tree
we will have a stand
all in white, presents on
& around it & after any
one places things there
they cant look or handle
them until the proper time
Send me a xmas card to
go in the corner, I would
appriciate it. Last month
I went to good old Wyandot
Co & stayed 2 weeks. Oh what
a change in 3 9 years.
as it had been that long
since I was there.

6.

6th I visited all of my child
hood homes, towns &.
Was at your old home
& the grave yard is all in
a field under big trees where
the horses & cattle stands
to fight flies. Many old
friends & school mates
are gone, the ones that
were left are few in
N. & said I looked so
young for my age. I
am very busy making
garments for presents to
send to Ala also to give
to some poor children
here in town. & Widows.

7.

7th I must tell
you what for a trick I am
playing on John. He has
been talking of making or
bying a Phonograph record
cabinet, & I knew he could
not make one with the
tools he had. So we L.C. &
me spoke to a good Carpen
& found the lumber & took
it to him when John was
gone, & he is now making
it according to order, I talk
around (you know I can do)
& found out about what he
wanted. L.C. is helping
they only have nights
& Satur days to work at it
We will have that in the

8.

8th corner too. Now Lena
I will tell you of a few
of the presents I have for
the home Children, One
is a good warm blanket
all wool, another a wash
boiler, a nice kettle to cook
in. A flannel shirt, a pair
of warm shoes for Mother
baker. She lives in Ind
we expect to go a see
her just after Xmas. She
is 81 & very poorly, I have
already baked 30 mince
pies. I always count the no
of mince I bake. We have
butchered 3 hogs. Now I cant
tell how well we would

128

9.

You can save money six days out of the week by trading at
THE WAUGH SHOE STORE,
31 Public Square, LIMA, OHIO.

[handwritten:] love to come in some day & see you & eat some of Lizzies good dinners. Now don't think of any thing else next summer spring as soon to come & see your oldly Aunt One that loves all of you dear Children. Ellens Childrens will bee with us xmas but Haldabel wont. Keep this letter & let all read it that desires. Till Willie & Lennie to read it whether they wants or not. ha ha & you people will have to read to see what is in it. then you will think

10.

[handwritten:] not after all. I have wrote to all of you children since I saw you & none have answered but Andy J. I think lots of Lawsons wife, I must write to them soon. She seems to think every thing of Aunt Moll & Unkle John. Now Lottie I am about to quit talking to you for this time. Wont some of you answer this & keep up your courage ask the Lord to help you & Aunt Moll will pray for you that you may be restored to your usual health & pray for your self & give your heart to God &c.

From Aunt Moll & John.

Notes on Aunt Moll's letter

Page 6: The graveyard she mentions is the graveyard that was reserved when David sold the property to George Kear in 1867.

Page 9: Ellen, mentioned on page nine is her sister, Sarah Ellen Doud. Apparently Ellen lived in Wyandot or an adjoining county. No record of her marriage or family has been found and this was the first reference about her after her name was listed in Harriet Higbie's book. See Chapter Four.

Page 10: She also says, "I have wrote to all of you children since I saw you and none have answered but Andy J. I think lots of Lawson's wife. She seems to think everything of Aunt Moll and Uncle John." This last sentence indicates that Roger Lawson Banfield was married by 1909, a fact not known earlier.

It has been a challenge to follow the life of Roger Lawson Banfield. He was not living with a Murray or a Banfield family in the 1900 census, but there was an

I.W. or L.W. Banfield living with the Charley Walters family in Polk County, Missouri. Because he reported his age as twenty-four and his half-brother Louis Banfield was living in Polk County, this census record appears to be Roger Lawson Banfield.

In the 1910 census of Raton City, New Mexico, a Robert L. Banfield, age 33, born in Missouri, was living with his wife, Allie. Their children were Gladys age 7, Bernice age 2 and Urban age 1. Robert was an engineer with the railroad.

Roger L. Banfield's World War I registration was made in Tucumcari, New Mexico. His closest relative was his wife Allie and he was an engineer with the railroad.

The 1930 census of Quay, New Mexico listed a Lawson C. Banfield, divorced, working as locomotive engineer. He stated that his father was born in Tennessee and his mother was born in Ohio, which is correct. It is strange that he used the names Robert, Roger and Lawson in legal documents, but the information still indicates that these facts relate to Roger Lawson Banfield.

His death certificate from New Mexico stated that Roger Lawson Banfield died 20 December, 1943. His occupation was listed as railroad engineer with the Southern Pacific Railroad. He was buried in the Tucumcari, New Mexico cemetery.

The Murray family had little contact with Uncle Lawson. He occasionally came to Greene County and visited with his half-brothers or their families. He maintained closer contact with Andy, perhaps because of the Banfield family relationship.

This picture of Z.G. and an unnamed man was taken in Lima, Ohio, where Aunt Moll and Uncle John lived. It indicated that families from Missouri and Ohio visited each other in the 1890s and early 1900s. The man in the picture may be Aunt Moll's husband or son.

In 1907 Zelotus wrote his sister Evaline about problems with his son, Luther. Apparently this letter was never mailed. Perhaps the family learned that Evaline and John Makely were having problems, because in her 1909 letter, Aunt Moll said, "I suppose you knew that John and Evaline was divorced." Lena no doubt wrote the letter for Z.G. because she says, "Lotes has gone and done for him all winter and he does not appreciate it at all."

1.

2.

3.

4.

In 1909 Z.G. received this letter from his sister, Evaline, asking for a loan of $15. She said that "John has went off to the bad and left Marie and I alone." She was supporting herself and Marie by sewing for $1.00 per day. This letter shows why Evaline could not help with her brother's request to find work for Luther.

1.

2.

3.

4.

Apparently Zelotus' daughter Evaline, agreed to help her brother Luther. Evaline had married Baker Owen and Luther is listed in their household in the 1910 census of Polk County, Missouri. Luther's occupation was listed as "hired out."

Luther was convicted of felonious assault in Greene County, 23 February, 1907. The charge was that on 23 November, 1906, "Luther Murray did feloniously assault Cloys Burney by cutting said Burney with a knife giving him a wound of 2 inches, depth of 3 inches." A guilty verdict was punishable by 2-10 years in Missouri State Penitentiary. The final judgment on 5 April, 1907, was: "Jury found defendant guilty of felonious assault w/intent to kill or do bodily harm without malice aforethought and assess his punishment at $100." Signed, W.E. Gidion, foreman. Lena's letter to Evaline indicated that Z.G. had two friends on the jury who saved Luther from the penitentiary sentence.

Luther settled down, married Maud Tiller on 18 January, 1911, and lived on his farm until 1947. He died following injuries when a truck fell on him while he was repairing it.

Many receipts were found for insurance policies on the dwelling and on personal property. Z.G. insured his property with the Farmers' Mutual Fire Insurance Company of Billings, Missouri for many years. Following is a sample of losses paid out and names of individuals receiving compensation. Many of the names are well known in Greene County. Because the insurance company was a mutual company, the policy holder could expect to receive a pro rata assessment due after losses had been paid. Z.G.'s assessment due on 15 February, 1910, was $3.83.

Although several banks were incorporated in Springfield in the early 1900s, many people continued borrowing money from their friends and relatives. Money moved from person to person depending on the

Springfield
Aug 19-1905-
Mr. Murray.
Dear Sir I would like to borrow about $700 for one year or may be longer will give good note come in tomorrow.
Frank B. Evans.

No. 10,074
THE McDANIEL NATIONAL BANK

OFFICERS
H. L. SCHNEIDER, President
W. T. BAUER, Vice President
GEO. D. McDANIEL, Cashier
JOHN T. YOUNG, Assistant Cashier

CAPITAL STOCK $100,000.00

DIRECTORS
H. L. SCHNEIDER
ALVA B. HILLIDAN
J. B. MONTGOMERY
L. E. LINES
W. T. BAUER
JOHN T. YOUNG
GEO. D. ANSLINGER
GERTRUDE B. McDANIEL
C. B. McAFEE
W. I. DIFFENDERFFER
GEO. D. McDANIEL

Springfield, Mo. Aug. 21, 1912.

Mr. Z. G. Murray,
City.

Dear Sir:

Mr. Chas. W. Tooker left with us to-day for you check for $90.00. The first time you are in town, if you will call around we will give it to you.

Very respectfully,

_____ Cashier.

A. W. OLLIS & CO.,
REAL ESTATE INVESTMENTS,
FARM, FRUIT, TIMBER AND MINERAL LANDS, AND MINING PROPERTIES.
214 WEST COMMERCIAL STREET.

SPRINGFIELD, MO.,

April 7th, 1910.

Mr. Z. G. Murray,
Springfield, Missouri, Route #5.

Dear Sir:

We have an application for a $1000 loan for five years on 86 acres belonging to E. S. Burrow. The land is described as follows: 30 acres in the N E of S W of Sec 12-30-23, all fenced, 20 acres in cultivation and with 3 room house; also 56 acres, part of the South one-half of N E of Sec 7-30-22 in Robberson Township, lying just South of Hackney P. O. This last tract is all bottom, 27 acres in cult but no other improvements. The first mentioned tract is in Cass Twp, lying West of Hackney, P. O. We wish to know if you would make an inspection of this property, tomorrow, if possible, and decide if you would be interested in making Mr. Burrow this loan. If not kindly advise us at once and oblige.

Very truly,

A.W. Ollis & Co.

urgency of the individual's financial need. Interest rates were six, eight and ten percent.

In 1910, Ollis Real Estate Company was located on Commercial Street, and from the details printed on their letterhead, the company dealt exclusively with commercial real estate. Today it is in business as an insurance agency located on East Sunshine Street. In this letter, A.W. Ollis asked if Z.G. would loan money on a farm located at Hackney on Sac River.

On 26 July, 1910, Z.G. received a letter from G.F. Berry, a representative of Ozark Land Company, telling him about a buyer for the Murray farm. He stated: "Not many men would tackle a $16,000 proposition like this and he is just the kind of a fellow that is not afraid."

Z.G. must have been interested in the proposition because he made a list of livestock and machinery which he would be willing to sell: mares, mules, horse wagons, a mower and sulkey rake, bull rake, binder, corn planter, wheat drill, planter, cultivators, plows, 500 feet of oak and walnut, and corn, oats and hay. He also requested to reserve from the sale the half an acre where the graveyard was located.

There are no family stories about why the sale did not go through. Zelotus' son, Dorsey, recalled that there was a dispute at some time when Lena objected to a sale of the property and chased an individual out of the house with a butcher knife in her hand. Lena never wanted to sell the farm and passed that sense to her descendants. Perhaps because of her German background, she knew the importance of land ownership.

On 13 January, 1913, Zelotus G. Murray died intestate. His Missouri Death Certificate listed the cause of death as pneumonia, with fatty degeneration as a secondary contributing cause. The inventory of his estate revealed a list of notes payable at six and eight percent interest. When workers received fifty cents a day for their wages and a railway ticket cost five dollars to go to the World's Fair, one wonders how men of means accumulated $2,000 and $5,000 to put out on loan.

On page 136, there is a list of loans payable to Z.G. which were part of the assets shown in his probate file.

Lena, who had been the wife of a successful farmer, found herself as the head of her family in charge of dividing an estate between herself and six children. She joined the women in previous generations who were suddenly left to deal with financial problems.

Zelotus' older children were married and the three younger children were minors. The older ones wanted and needed their inheritances. Susan had

No. 10,074

THE McDANIEL NATIONAL BANK

OFFICERS
H. L. SCHNEIDER, PRESIDENT
W. T. BRUER, VICE PRESIDENT
GEO. D. McDANIEL, CASHIER
JOHN T. YOUNG, ASSISTANT CASHIER

CAPITAL STOCK
$100,000.00

UNDER GOVERNMENT SUPERVISION

DIRECTORS
H. L. SCHNEIDER
ALVA D. MILLIGAN
J. B. MONTGOMERY
L. C. LINES
W. T. BRUER
JOHN T. YOUNG
GEO. D. ANSLINGER
GERTRUDE B. McDANIEL
C. B. McAFEE
W. L. DIFFENDERFFER
GEO. D. McDANIEL

Springfield, Mo. Feby 12—1

Cash in McDaniel Bank	$ 439.65
Watter, R. Chapman Jan 2—13 Note	5,000.00
interst	39.3
J.W. + F. M. Newton Note	2,200.00
interest	92.4
Edward M Weatherspoon Note	900.
interst	15.93
Jefferson D + F. M Newton Note	2,000.
interst	47.2
L. J. + W. C. R. J. Freeman Nat.	7,000.0
interst	86.
Levi + H. J. Trantham	200.0
interst	17
W. S. + J. S. Kissock	3,000.0
interst	234.5

No. 10,074

THE McDANIEL NATIONAL BANK

OFFICERS
H. L. SCHNEIDER, PRESIDENT
W. T. BRUER, VICE PRESIDENT
GEO. D. McDANIEL, CASHIER
JOHN T. YOUNG, ASSISTANT CASHIER

CAPITAL STOCK
$100,000.00

UNDER GOVERNMENT SUPERVISION

DIRECTORS
H. L. SCHNEIDER
ALVA D. MILLIGAN
J. B. MONTGOMERY
L. C. LINES
W. T. BRUER
JOHN T. YOUNG
GEO. D. ANSLINGER
GERTRUDE B. McDANIEL
C. B. McAFEE
W. L. DIFFENDERFFER
GEO. D. McDANIEL

Springfield, Mo. Feby 12—13

Elton Cooper Note	1000.00
Interst	71.83
William G + Lula D Gurby	600.00
interst	49.10
Elyzabeth Jane White Note	200.00
Interst	3.81
Farris H + Eura Newton Note	3,000.00
interst	184.92
Wheat 1021 Bu	981.75
8 School Bonds $50.00 each	400.00
interst	20.77

married Hosea Putman in 1901, Evaline had married Baker Owen in 1903 and Luther had married Maud Tiller in 1911. On 22 September, 1913, Lena entered into a warranty deed with Susan and her husband, Evaline and her husband, Luther and his wife, to purchase their rights to the farm for a total of $7350.

Walter, Dorsey and Mamie Murray

Lena's three children remained on the farm until Walter married Robbie Fallin in 1915 and Mamie married Gabe Sneed in 1916. Mamie and Walter conveyed their inheritance to their mother for $1 "love and affection." Walter and Dorsey worked together farming and helped Lena manage the farm. Walter pitched in and helped Lena when Dorsey was called to the military in 1917. Dorsey and Lena lived together until Lena married a neighbor, Teed Gurley. Lena died in 1945 and was buried with Z.G. at Greenlawn Cemetery, Springfield, Missouri.

A large family reunion was held after 1913 and before 1917 when World War I began. Matching census records with approximate ages of the young people pictured above, it appears that the photo must have been taken

Front row: Rome (Jerome) Owen, husband of Ollie Murray; Baker Owen, husband of Evaline Murray; Walter Murray; Carl Murray; Dorsey Murray; two unknown children; Janie or Jennie Murray, widow of William Murray; Melvin, Cornelia and Gene Owen, children of Ralph and Edna Owen; Maud Tiller Murray; Zelma Putman, daughter of Susan and Hosea Putman.

Second row: Three unknown men; Andy J. Murray; George Sterling; Rolen Sell (with star); unknown boy; unknown three women and three children; Lena Brune Murray (in black); Norman and Maizie Murray (children of William Murray); Edna and Ralph Owen; Luther Murray (standing behind his wife Maud); Hosea Putman and Susan Murray Putman.

Third row: Ezenith Sell; Elizabeth, wife of George Sterling; Lucy Jane Carter Murray; Ollie Murray Owen; unknown woman; unknown woman; unknown woman holding child; unknown man; Mamie Murray (Sneed); Jettie Murray (Cook); others in the row unknown.

There is some discrepancy between names marked on the photo and names mentioned above. Another relative marked those names and some are incorrect.

in 1914 or 1915. It is possible that it was taken in 1914 because Lena was still wearing black, possibly still in mourning following the death of Z.G. The labeled photograph identifies those descendants known at this time.

Another reunion apparently occurred in Ohio. It shows Rolen and Ezenith Sell, Andy and Lucy Jane Murray and Jerema's son, George and his family. The photo was probably taken the summer of 1918 because John J. Sterling enrolled in the Army 26 June, 1918.

First row: Ezenith Murray Sell, Lucy Jane Carter Murray, Elizabeth Sterling, Catherine D. Sterling, Lyndus Sterling.

Second row: Herald Sterling, Rolen Sell, Andy Murray, George Sterling, George Sterling Jr., and John J. Sterling.

After World War I, everything changed. Members of the older generation died and their children gradually lost contact with each other.

In 1929 the Great Depression began. Individuals stood in long lines to withdraw money from their banks and by 1933 thousands of banks had closed their doors. Farmers were hit hard because of falling food prices made worse by the devastating drought in Oklahoma, Texas and Kansas. Those states would later be called the Dust Bowl. Farmers in the Midwest looked up from their ploughing and saw dark clouds of dust rolling toward their farms. Their wives cleaned thick coats of dust from the furniture.

This Great Depression was worse than the Panic of '57 or the Panic of 1873, but the descendants of David Murray in Greene County weathered the depression. They were farmers so there was always food available, although not much disposable income. When the depression ended with the beginning of World War II, they sent their sons to fight in Germany and Japan.

Because of the depression and World War II, family members had no time for reunions. Family history was forgotten.

10

The Great War

This story could have ended with Zelotus G. Murray and his family, except that one small box was found in the family trunk. It was labeled "Souvenirs of 1917-1918." Grandma Lena saved Dorsey's letters, pictures and postcards during the time he served in World War I. He never talked about the war or his experiences and his letters were unread for years. Only after reading the history of the 89th Division and placing his letters with the history, did his experience come alive.

The United States entered the First World War on 6 April, 1917, totally unprepared for war, but convinced that the cause was right and that it was the war "to end all wars."

In a patriotic address before the Cotton States Merchants' Association Annual Convention, August 21, 1917, the Hon. Joseph W. Folk stated: "The American people are united as never before in a stern and resolute purpose...No good American can question the justice of our entering the war with Germany, unless he be ignorant of why we did so. We have viewed for years the preparations for war being made by Germany, little dreaming that they might concern us..." He continued, "Then came the sinking of the *Lusitania* and the wanton murder by drowning of hundreds of noncombatant American men and helpless women and children."

The public was ready and the government called up young men to register for the draft. Young men living on farms asked for exemptions because they feared that they might lose their land if no one could work on their farms.

Dorsey Murray was living with his mother, Lena, and he too, asked for an exemption. He received a letter on 28 August, 1917, denying his request.

Dorsey was inducted into the Army on 18 September, 1917, and sent to Camp Funston, Kansas. He became a private in the 342nd Field Artillery, 89th Division, which was organized on 5 September, 1917.

Local Board for the County of Greene
State of Missouri,
Local Board Springfield, Mo.

Serial No. *1319*

Address ....

(Insert designation by stamp according to sec. 3 of Regulations.)

Form No. 148, prepared by the Provost Marshal General.

NOTICE OF CERTIFICATION TO DISTRICT BOARD WHEN CLAIM OF EXEMPTION
OR DISCHARGE HAS BEEN DENIED.

To *Dorsie L. Murray*
(Name.)

Springfield Mo. R45
(Address.)

You are hereby notified that you were, on the ...*28th*... day of *August*......

191..., certified by this Local Board to District Board *Div. no. 2, West Jud. Div.* as
(Here insert designation in accordance with sec. 33 of Regulations.)

having been called for the military service of the United States, and not exempted or discharged, your

claim for ~~exemption~~—discharge—having been, by this Local Board, on the ...*28th*... day of
(Specify which.)

...*August*..., denied.

If you have filed a claim of exemption or discharge with this Local Board which has been denied, you may, according to the provisions of sec. 26 of the Rules and Regulations prescribed by the President under and pursuant to the act approved on the 18th day of May, 1917, claim an appeal from the decision of this Local Board denying your claim of exemption or discharge to said District Board to which you have been certified: *Provided,* That your claim of appeal is filed at the office of this Local Board within 10 days after the day on which this notice was mailed to you, and a notice of the filing of such claim of appeal to such District Board on a form provided by the Local Board is filed with said District Board within said period of 10 days.

If you are prevented by necessary absence or because of illness from filing your claim of appeal within said period, this Board may, in its discretion, allow you to file a claim of appeal after the expiration of said 10 days, provided you show to the satisfaction of the Board that you were so prevented by necessary absence or illness.

Your claim of appeal must be made on a form prepared by the Provost Marshal General which you may procure on application at the office of this Local Board.

Under the act of Congress approved May 18, 1917, each District Board has original, exclusive jurisdiction to hear and determine in respect of persons whose names have been certified to it by any Local Board as called for service and not exempted or discharged, all questions or claims for including or excluding or discharging such person arising under the following provisions of the said act authorizing the President to exclude or discharge "persons engaged in industries, including agriculture, found to be necessary to the maintenance of the Military Establishment, or the effective operation of the military forces, or the maintenance of national interest during the emergency."

Any claim for discharge upon this ground must be filed with the *District Board* to which the name of the claimant has been certified, upon a form prepared by the Provost Marshal General (Form No. 161 or No. 161a), which will be supplied by the District Boards or Local Boards, on or before the *fifth* day after the mailing by a Local Board of this notice that your name has been certified to such District Board as called for service and not exempted or discharged.

Local Board for the County of Greene
State of Missouri,
Local Board .... Springfield, Mo.

By ....
(Chairman.)

....
(Clerk.)

N. B.—The date of the mailing of this notice is the ...*28th*... day of ...*August*..., 191 *7*

8—4024

A posting on the internet detailed the history of the 342nd Field Artillery. It was written by Lt. C.J. Hansen, who served in the 342nd. His recollections were written in 1919. The letters which Dorsey wrote paralleled the history which Lt. Hansen wrote. It seemed appropriate to borrow from Lt. Hansen's history and insert Dorsey's letters. Although his letters were not detailed about war activities, (Dorsey was never a man of many words) they do give a personal touch to the history narrative. In order to credit Lt. Hansen's words, they will be placed in italics.

The 342nd Field Artillery was organized September 5th, 1917, at Camp Funston, Kansas, under the command of Colonel George A. Nugent, U.S.N.A. The regiment was recruited from the first draft of men from Green, Polk, Dallas, Stone, Bollinger, and Laclede counties of southeastern Missouri, men for the most part from farms and rural communities. (Lt. Hansen did not realize that only Bollinger County is located in southeastern Missouri; the other counties are located in southwestern Missouri.)

By the end of September, the short space of three weeks, the regiment had enrolled 145 men, very nearly filling its quota. Meanwhile, building construction of the camp was keeping pace with the increase in troops and before the end of the month the regiment had moved into a second set of temporary quarters in the 16th Unit, where most of the fourteen hundred men were received, bathed, clothed and examined. Just how the cold showers, the ill-fitting uniforms, and the strange routine of roll calls, foot drill, mess, and more foot drill impressed the men is for future reminiscences.

Dorsey wrote: "Well, our company won in a platoon drill. They picked out the best drilled men and I was in it. We have got a good Captain and Lutenant."

Certainly there was novelty in the rapidly changing surroundings, with soldiers drilling among lumber scrap piles, along the dusty streets of completed cantonments, or again on the scarcely trodden prairie grass of the flats.

Postcard dated November 15, 1917.

The problem of equipment was a difficult one.... (The men) were directed to making wooden rifles for simulation of manual arms, for as yet there had been no rifles received and even the guard carried only wooden clubs. The regiment was organized as a dismounted motorized heavy artillery outfit, 6-inch or 155 mm. Howitzer; so that while training, no motor equipment was available.

The next few months passed slowly for this regiment of motorless, gunless, motorized artillery. The only equipment received consisted of U.S. Model 1917 rifles, and all artillery training was necessarily theoretical.

Fort Riley and Junction City

Community House for Soldiers and Citizens

This building, erected by the citizens of Junction City, is dedicated to the use of the Soldiers and Citizens of Junction City and Fort Riley with the hope that here may be formed many pleasant and lasting friendships.

Junction City, Kans., Oct 13 1917

Best wishes to you all:

Saturday eve oct 13 - 17

It is just eigh know I have plenty of time have to be back by eleven. We take a motor car its about eigh mi to camps. I sent mamm a card when I first got here dont guess she got it. When yours get any thing good to eat send me some. Clarence is writing to Jettie think he writes every time he goes to a town. How is every thing getting along you nedent to worry iff you couldnt get any one to work it isint like staying at that dry old camp Funston when the wind blows you cant see hardly for the dust. Got a letter from Carl the other day. I want to get a furlough iff I can fath non of us boys have tryed yet. From Dorsey murray.

Dorsey referred to his buddy, Clarence Knox, who was writing to Jettie Murray, Dorsey's first cousin. Carl, referred to in the letter, is Jettie's brother.

The holiday season was duly celebrated. On the afternoon of Thanksgiving Day the regiment marched in a body to an inter-divisional football game. Christmas was marked by similar feats and more athletic events.

This looks like a tug-of-war.

Dorsey wrote: "Scene of wild west riders on Xmas day Camp Funston Kansas."

Dorsey wrote: "These boys were out on a rabbit hunt. I didn't get to go along as I was busy. They belong to HQ Co. though."

This was a trophy won by Headquarters Company, 342 Field Artillery. Real guns must have arrived at the camp.

The December record was marred by considerable sickness throughout the Division, and the regiment lost fourteen men by death, largely from pneumonia. This began a series of quarantines that were occasionally imposed upon the regiment for mumps, measles and meningitis.

NATIONAL WAR WORK COUNCIL OF
YOUNG MEN'S CHRISTIAN ASSOCIATIONS
OF THE UNITED STATES
"WITH THE COLORS"

Camp Funston Feb 16 1918

Hello Mama. How are you all. I am all right. We have been having some pretty nice weather with the exception of one or two days. You know when the wind blows it is just some thing awful how dusty it is. Clarence is still over at the hospital guess he must have the mumps. Well I havent taken them yet. But I can't tell how soon I may for I have been right with them for more than a month. Say that sure is me like some price for them three year old mules. Do you think you will need them next spring. Let me know whether or not they would stay that high it might pay

NATIONAL WAR WORK COUNCIL OF
YOUNG MEN'S CHRISTIAN ASSOCIATIONS
OF THE UNITED STATES
"WITH THE COLORS"

Feb 16 – 1918

to keep them. They shurley have growed some since I saw them. I hear that Ray Sprinkle is in the next call it won't leave very many boys if they keep on drafting them. Carl was lucky to get in the second class. I am sending you one of my pictures, I didn't think I needed a shave so bad till I saw these pictures, ah well they will do.

From Dorsey.

Dorsey referred to Carl, his first cousin, son of Andrew J. Murray.

Scenes from the barracks and mess hall. At left, Dorsey identifies himself "me."

NATIONAL WAR WORK COUNCIL OF
YOUNG MEN'S CHRISTIAN ASSOCIATIONS
OF THE UNITED STATES

"WITH THE COLORS"

Camp Fuston Feb 24 - 1918

Hello Mama, How are you
I am well. I received the
box you sent yesterday.
It was fine. Glad to get
them from home. For it
might be some day so I couldn't
get a box from home. You
know they are transferring the
boys all the time and I
don't know when I will be
next. We boys have begin
to think we are going
abroad some of these days.
Some new drafted boys came
in yesterday evening and they
keep sending out a few all
the time. If we get out
of quarentee before I am transfered
will probably get a pass. If I
don't I think I will take one
any way. You needent go to any

NATIONAL WAR WORK COUNCIL OF
YOUNG MEN'S CHRISTIAN ASSOCIATIONS
OF THE UNITED STATES

"WITH THE COLORS"

Feb 24 - 1918

trouble of sending me a
box every week for I am
still working in the kitchen
for I know it is extra work
and trouble for you and Robbie
Have you ever heard of Fred. I
Carl heard he was in New Jersey
and havent heard from him
since then. The weather is
fine out here allmost like
summertime I have been
out bumming around this
morning been over to the depo
me and a boy by the name of
he is from Springfield and was
in the bunch that was to be
transferred but he didnt get
to go with the boys and was
sent back to the Company.
me, Carl and Clarence went over
to army city last night. This is

Fensons newest town
has been built since this
camp was built. We boys go
to a show now and then and
that is about all we do to pass
the time off. Well by now
doubt the time has past by
pretty fast for it is getting
pretty close to spring now.
Has Walter ploughed any ground
yet for oats. Gee. that is
some price for them mules!
$$$ I believe that is all
they are worth of course
I wouldnt say to sell
them for they must be a find
team. That one I imagine will
be hard to break but iff they
are broke good they will make
a good team. How are the sheep
doing. Will close From Dorcy.

Due to the carefully arranged system of distribution and efficient provisions for clothing and feeding the men, the first five per cent of the draft was inducted into the service without severe hardship.

To represent Camp Funston as a mere training ground, and the regiment as six batteries and two companies would be to omit a real description of the life there. Passes were liberally distributed and the men were given much liberty in visiting nearby towns. The "Y" and later the "Zone" served to furnish recreation.

When the regiment left Camp Funston on June 3rd, 1918, it was considerably below strength, having contributed an average of 100 men a month to replacement detachments during the previous five months.

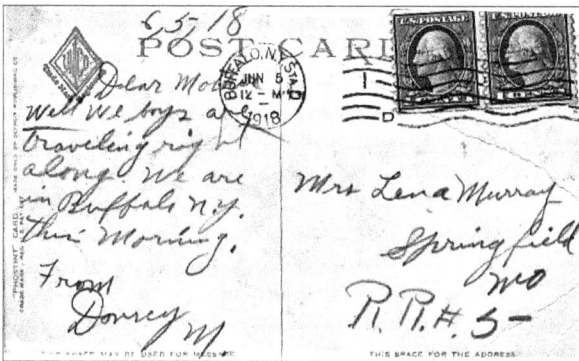

Dorsey did not write about his trip from New York to England and only commented on his post card that "everything was looking pretty and green" in England.

Disembarking at about 5:00 o'clock the regiment marched through Liverpool to the debarkation camp at Knotty Ash, a tent camp apparently built in a private estate or park. After a comfortable night at Knotty Ash there was another hike and we entrained for Winchester. The morning of July 12th found us again on the march to entrain for Southhampton. A short wait at the docks gave us opportunity to look over a park of artillery materiel, captured or condemned, and to take a good look at the ships, most of which bore heavy scars of submarine encounters or displayed gaping holes where torpedoes had torn through. It was a bad night. When the regiment lined up finally on the docks at LeHarve, it was a very tired organization.

Soldiers were given a thank you letter from King George expressing "God speed on your mission." This letter must have been written in April 1918 and given to all servicemen.

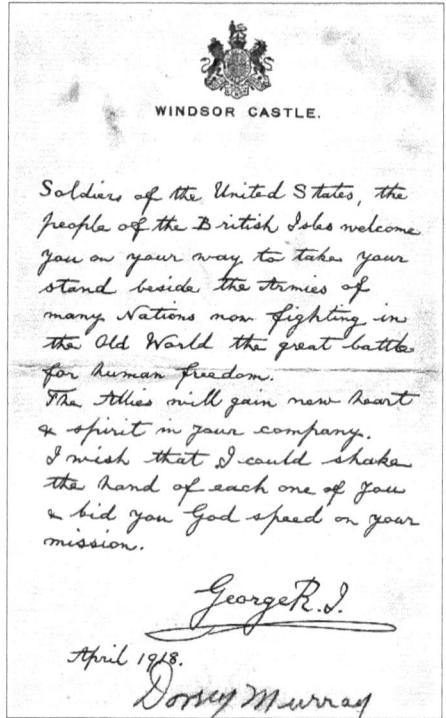

WINDSOR CASTLE.

Soldiers of the United States, the people of the British Isles welcome you on your way to take your stand beside the Armies of many Nations now fighting in the Old World the great battle for human freedom.

The Allies will gain new heart & spirit in your company. I wish that I could shake the hand of each one of you & bid you God speed on your mission.

George R.I.

April 1918.

Dorsey Murray

6 BORDEAUX. — Les Allées de Tourny. — Tourny Walk. — LL.

Bastille Day found the 342nd F.A., A.E.F., marching in pouring rain through the streets of LeHarve (France) to entrain for parts unknown. We soon learned from our interpreters, who joined us here, that our station was to be somewhere near Bordeaux. With occasional stops for coffee and water we crept slowly south through western France to Bordeaux, and on July 16th, detrained at St. Medard, Gironde, and hiked some eight kilometers to the town of LeTaillan.

Here we received the battery of the guns we were finally to use—1915 model Schneider 155 mm howitzer and both officers and men settled down to master the drill and service of the piece. About a week after we arrived, we learned definitely, and for the first time, that we were to be a horse-drawn regiment...Altho we had always been skeptical of ever receiving any tractors and motors, this was something of a surprise, for all our training had been for motor tractors. However, thanks to the farmers of the regiment, there were plenty of men who were at home with horses and mules. As one man from old Missouri expressed it, "I ain't done nothing all my life, only drive mules."

Hello to all   August 2, 18   In France

Dear Mother. How are you all, I am all right. It has been trying to rain here. Has it ever rained back there yet this is about the time of the year for it to be dry. It has been pretty hot here but not so hot as it is back home. Have you all threshed yet, I guess you have by now and all most ready for fall ploughing. Which make the best wheat at home or the Mullings place, I still have some U.S. money and I think I will keep it. It looks good to the side of this French money.

.   Will close from Dorsey M

Of all the regiment's experiences in France the stay at Taillan was perhaps the most pleasant. Since we were the first American troops to be billeted in this town, the inhabitants took the opportunity to give us a hearty welcome. On August 3, the regiment left Le Taillan for the barracks at Camp de Souge and commenced the six weeks' strenuous course at the School of Fire. Telephone, radio, machine gun and reconnaissance officers and details took practical courses and drivers and cannoneers had their first actual experience in handling a battery. Such excellent progress was made by the Brigade that we completed the final, big problem a week in advance and received official commendation from the Director of the School.....we were soon cautioned to prepare to move...

Walter is Dorsey's brother.
Mazie is his cousin, daughter
of William Murray and Gussie
is Lena's nephew. Dorsey's
frequent comments about
ploughing and harvesting show
that he was thinking of home,
and perhaps, a little homesick.

On very short notice the Regiment moved out. Due to plentiful room and the use of rolling kitchens for hot food, the trip was more comfortable than that from LeHarve. The first section (Headquarters) arrived at Toul about noon of September 18th and immediately took the road for a forced march through Lucey, Menil-La-Tour, Flirey and Essey to Pannes, where regimental headquarters was established.

Once established on the front in the "quiet sector", the regiment began to settle down to the routine of firing at night and working during the day, sleeping between times. Tho our areas were shelled periodically, the first impression of an

LIBERTY BONDS WILL KEEP THESE HOWITZERS THUNDERING AT THE HUNS

artilleryman's life at the front was less danger and more plain hard labor. Carrying 100-lb shells up to the guns, washing and greasing them, and fuzing and firing at night left little time to worry about anything but food and sleep. The German dugouts we adopted and improved, and after a shell or two landed in our neighborhood, we also began to develop some fair excavations.

In the course of time, however the receipt of orders over the phone, the assignment of missions, the rousing of the officers and calculations of data became a common-place, and usually within fifteen minutes after receipt of an order the men were out, lighting devices set, and the first shell over. "Rounds complete" became merely a grateful signal for the men to curl up in their blankets and fall asleep, just as though hurling a few tons (more or less) of high explosive across miles of country had been a custom for years in the Ozarks.

Although frequent short bursts of reprisal fire were directly ordered and occasional raids took place, the first three weeks in October were very quiet. This was due to a variety of causes. By an order of Oct. 5th it was announced that the supply of ammunition was low in this sector and that batteries would keep strictly within their allowance.

On the third of November information was received indicating a withdrawal by the enemy along the entire front. The first battalion of the 342nd was in support of the left, laying down destructive fire on the point of attack and then shifting forward to neutralize machine guns beyond the Hindenburg line.

Nov 4, 18.

Dear Mother. How are you? I am faring just fine. We just moved to a new home some of the boys are living in build. But I happen to make my

...another boy as to operate the switch board during the night. We have a fine dug out, it has a concrete floor in it, and has logs on the sides and over head. We have our stove and a fine bunk. It is all Fritzes Property. He had things fixed up pretty good all kinds of furniture just as handy as can be. Well I just received a letter from Walter today but as I haddent answered your letter yet he will have to wait.

Well I here isnt much to write of all though the papers have good news and of course you all get that. We get the N.Y. paper here all most every day. I have only received three ...... so far. Well I guess you are having some pretty bad weather there now. Walter is getting along with the ...... serving fine and to know he is having as much as he is sounds good I guess we will have some good fall pasture over at the Mullings Place I hear that they have the influenzia all most every place, that shure is bad. That was too bad about Luther Baby I didn't even know it was sick. over

As Baby .... very much .... heat. I am getting lazy here lately we have bjen having it pretty easy I only work from twelve till six at night. I get kinda tired getting around to be back to work a little. Well I think we would be back before many months iff things continue as they are. Say I will send you some of this French money next time I write. one franc or two

Will close from
Dorsey

Luther was Dorsey's half-brother, the son of Z.G. and Maggie. His son, Clay, was nine months old when he died from influenza, during the influenza pandemic of 1918.

Reconnaissance was assigned to the 112th Infantry for the early hours of November 10th. At 5:30 that morning a battalion advanced with the mission of penetrating the salient near Dommartin, capturing prisoners and determining the strength of the enemy. Opening fire at the H hour the 342nd fired for two hours on targets in the vicinity of Dommartin and Dampvitoux, with irregular volleys of harassing fire. Due to the method of fire only about 900 rounds were expended by the 155's. During the night of Nov 10 the regiment fire a total of 2472 rounds.

Following the armistice on the 11th, and the constant firing that preceded the cessation of hostilities, the natural inclination of everyone was to take a few hours rest. The artillery remained for a week or so in the dugouts of the positions and then gradually moved to the slightly more comfortable quarters afforded by the ruined towns.

The Second Battalion moved batteries, echelon and Headquarters into the town of Beney on the 17th, while the Third Battalion made the best of quarters in Bouillonville.

The announcement that the 89th Division was part of the Army of Occupation was shortly followed by orders to take the road to join our Division. Extra horses had been drawn and on the morning of November 29th the regiment took the road for Germany. We found pioneers and engineers still engaged in blowing up the mines in the vicinity. On the next days march it was something of a relief to leave the ruins of the war zone.

On December 1st with fair weather and good roads a trip to Xivray-Circourt (Hq.2nd and 3rdBn) and to Merc7-le-bas for the first battalion was an easy march and there was time to spare to clean up equipment and materiel.

The route of march on December 3rd took the regiment through the industrial towns of Longwy and Mt. St. Martin. Crossing the Belgian border at Aubange, we continued to Messancy, where we were billeted for the night. Here the people appeared far different from those in northern France, having enough food and still retaining most of their livestock. The next day we left Belgium—bear Arlon and entered wooded country in Luxemburg.

The eighth day out brought us through the most interesting country of the trip and into the most ancient of the towns...suddenly down into the valley of the Sauer River, where Vianden was located.

Here the regiment had a pleasant stay. In the evening a civilian band made the rounds of the town followed by the greater part of the population forming a torch-light procession.

France Nov 28, 18

Dear mother will try and write a few lines. It has been pretty rainy here lately. We haven't had anything to do to mount to anything since the armistice was signed looks like we would start home pretty soon. There has been rhumors that we were going to the German border.

I dont care much about the trip. Well in fact non of us boys do. We have been near Metz since sept 19, now at Benny. I guess Springfield put on quite a hurrah when the armistice was signed. I wrote walter a letter that day and that is the last one till this one. It seems like every time it is a little harder to write. We are not living in a dug out now But it isn't much better than one. the buildings are so old and torn up by the war. If we make that trip to Germany which is about 125 miles we will see lots more of France and probably Germany. Oh yes this is Thanksgiving day.

We boys are sitting by the fire having a chat now and then mentioning things back home. Mayie sent me some pictures taken at home they shure look natural. Will close

From Dorsey

Thanksgiving Day in France.

Left: Dorsey wrote: "We stayed overnight at this place Dec 6, 18. The German border is about a mile from it."

Right: Dorsey remarked after the war about how backward everyday life was in Europe. He couldn't believe that women still washed clothes in the river.

Leaving Vianden at 8 o'clock on December 7th, a quarter of an hour brought us across the German border. The townspeople showed us no hostility. As we found in all of the rural districts of the Rhineland, food was plentiful.

Having been constantly on the road during the previous nine days and having covered about 190 kilometers, the tenth day was spent in Oberweis and nearby towns in resting, cleaning up and reshoeing. On the 9th the regiment left Oberweis at 8 o'clock and marched through Bitburg...and through Erdorf, to Badem, Pickliessem, and Spangdahlem (Hq. and 2nd Bn.) in which towns the regiment was billeted for five days. The towns were dirty and inconvenient, and the orders for the subsequent move were fortunate for us.

Dec 10, 18 Germany

Dear Mother,
How are you. I am
all right. It has been
quite a while since
I wrote you but we
have been on the go
lately. We are now
in Germany at a
town called Sparg
It isn't much of a
town. We have been
on the go for about

eleven days. Most all
of us have hiked it
through we started
near Mety at a little
town called Benny. We
always stopped at a town
or a village rather it was
quite a thing we don't
know how long we
stay here when we
start home or any thing
about it. We came through
Belgium and Luxemburg
to Germany. They shure
gave us a hearty welcome
in Belgium and Luxemburg.
Well I guess they did. I
have quite a time at Spgf.
When the armistice was
signed. They shure done
some firing the night and
morning till the time
to cease firing.
Then all at once
things ceased at 11 am
then the boys come
in a hollering.
Don't know when
we will get back
in a couple months
I guess.
Will close
From Dorsy

On the 15th we retraced our march to Bitburg and then took the Echternoah road to Wolafeld...Aladorf...and Niederweiss...and Irrel. In these towns the regiment remained and celebrated the holiday season. No trouble was experienced with the inhabitants, and the Christmas and New Year celebrations were none the less merry for being spent in hostile territory.

Christmas in Germany.

The long march into Germany was accomplished without any unfortunate incident. No materiel was abandoned and only four animals were lost on the march. Very little was requisitioned from the inhabitants...the men were under cover every night, and never pitched shelter camps in the open, which was fortunate in view of the consistently wet weather experienced.

During January the regiment carried out a systematic training schedule. Occasional manoeuvres were held, and novelty was introduced into the training by the receipt of motors for the long postponed motorization of the regiment.

Wolsfeld Germany
Feb 10, 19

Dear Mother how are you all by now. I just received a letter from you this morning dated Jan 21, I well I know I neglect writing but as there is nothing much to write it makes it hard to write. Well it has been pretty cold here lately it has been snowing some lately.

There isnt much news as to when we will start home and we are all anxious to get started back. Thats all the boys say is when are we going home while all though the people here treat us good as they can. I was surprised at Mamie and Gabe buying a new place I dont guess I know where it is. well I will close from
Dorsey

Mamie is Dorsey's sister; Gabe is her husband.

Lt. Hansen's narrative ends with the above paragraph. The only additional notation was a memorandum to the 89th Division: "There are no members of this Regiment who have been awarded the Medal of Honor, Distinguished Service Cross, or Distinguished Service Medal." Signed, Robert B. Putnam, lst Lt. 342nd Field Artillery. Intelligence Officer. March 9th, 1919.

The troops settled in to wait for their trip back to the United States.

Dorsey wrote: "Arrived here Dec. 14."

Wolfeld Germany.
April 14, 19

Dear Brother:
Will try and write
you a few lines.
this evening it has
been raining most
all day here and
a little bit cooler
than usual. Well
as your letter I
just received seems
as though you are
getting along with
things very well
I always like to
read your letters as
to how things are about

oats sewed. How
do you like your
riding plough by
now. its a wonder
you would of bought
them. Well I don't
know when we
will start home
for shure but it
is in May or the
first of June.
Will close for
this time
with best wishes
to all. Dorsey M.

Dorsey Louis Murray

Dorsey's final letter was on 3 June, 1919. He was in New York, on his way to Camp Funston, Kansas for discharge.

Dorsey was discharged from the Army on 10 June, 1919, and returned to Springfield. He lived his life as a farmer and never wanted to travel again.

ENLISTMENT RECORD.

Name: *Dorsey L. Murray*   Grade: *Private*

Enlisted, or Inducted, *September 18*, 1917, at *Springfield Missouri*

Serving in *first* enlistment period at date of discharge.

Prior service: * *Entitled to wear two gold service chevrons*

Noncommissioned officer:

Marksmanship, gunner qualification or rating: *not rated*

Horsemanship: *Not Mounted*

Battles, engagements, skirmishes, expeditions: *Pannes Flirey sector Sept 18th Nov 11, 1918 :: Army of Occupation Nov 29 1918 to May 11, 1919*

Knowledge of any vocation: *Farmer*

Wounds received in service: *none*

Physical condition when discharged: *Good*

Typhoid prophylaxis completed *October 15, 1917 ; ICC-II Lipa Vacc 3/17/19*

Paratyphoid prophylaxis completed *October 15, 1917 ;*

Married or single: *single*

Character: *Excellent*

Remarks: *No "A.W.O.L" nor absence under G.O 45-14 nor 31-12. Entitled to reduced R.R. fare and travel pay to Springfield Missouri*

Signature of soldier: *Dorsey L. Murray*

Monroe C Lewis 1st Lieut, 342 F.C. Commanding 6th Bat.

Honorable Discharge from The United States Army

TO ALL WHOM IT MAY CONCERN:

This is to Certify, That* *Dorsey Louis Murray 1213 9410 Private Headquarters Co. 342 F. A.* THE UNITED STATES ARMY, as a TESTIMONIAL of HONEST and FAITHFUL SERVICE, is hereby HONORABLY DISCHARGED from the military service of the UNITED STATES by reason of *Instr F.O. 89th Div April 28, 1918* Said *Dorsey Louis Murray* was born in *Springfield*, in the State of *Missouri* When enlisted he was 21 ½ years of age and by occupation a *Farmer* He had *brown* eyes, *brown* hair, *fair* complexion, and was 5 feet 8 inches in height. *Given under my hand at Camp Funston, Kansas this 10th day of June, one thousand nine hundred and Nineteen*

Guy C Pollock Capt 342 F.A. Commanding

11

Closing The Trunk

The trunk is empty now, except for some clothing from the late 1890s. Z.G.'s black felt stockman's hat, sits on top of the pile. A great-grandmother's faded brown bonnet lies beside it—not a fancy bonnet, but one that she would wear while gardening. Dark green scrolls painted on the vanilla colored lining seem as bright as they must have been one hundred fifty years ago.

After combing through all the papers and spending years in research, I learned a lot about the family. I also found puzzles which will never be solved; the answers lie buried with the ancestors. Perhaps that is what they would want.

I have tried to be the story teller for the family. In a few generations no one will remember the great-grandparents. Family stories and legends will die. But one day, a young person will suddenly ask, "Who were my ancestors? Where did they come from?" Hopefully this book will answer questions about the ancestors' lives and the historic events they experienced.

This family is similar to so many others in the United States: an immigrant ancestor, sons who fought in wars, sons who invested their money and hard work in their communities, daughters who married and disappeared into their new families. It tells about the struggles of men and women who settled in the wilderness, survived illnesses, deaths of spouses and children, and major financial depressions. It is also a story of strong women, facing impossible odds to keep their families together. It is a part of the history of America.

My father was Dorsey. He would be embarrassed that I wrote about him and his family. He was a very private person who frequently asked the question, "What will the neighbors think?" I wondered if he learned that fear from his mother Lena, because individuals of German heritage were afraid that neighbors might question their loyalty during World War I.

Dorsey was a farmer, working long days, but allowing himself infrequent pleasures of fishing and bowling. He enjoyed socializing with his friends at the Presbyterian Church where he served as an elder. Otherwise, his life was fairly mundane. He frequently said there was no place as beautiful as the farm and he had no desire to travel unless it was to the lake for another fishing trip.

The picture above shows Dorsey with his brother, cousin, and neighborhood buddies. It was probably taken before he was married and after his Army service in World War I. Don't they look like a group of dandies?

Dorsey married Ama Giboney in 1925. She was a descendant of Alexander and Sarah Giboney, who settled in Greene County in 1845. They homesteaded the land which became Doling Park, containing the Giboney Cave, a Greene County Historic Site.

Ama Giboney Murray

I am their only child. My husband and I own the David Murray farm and maintain Huldah's house. The lane in front of the house and the house are on the Greene County Historic Sites Register; the lane designated because it was part of the original Boonville Road used by the Butterfield Overland Mail and the house because of its Italianate design, unusual for rural Greene County.

I have closed the trunk and closed the research on this family. The family members who tossed those letters, receipts and scraps of paper in the trunk, would never have believed that the papers would be saved for over a hundred years or that anyone might try to make sense of them. But those papers provided the clues that unraveled their stories. To those who saved these documents, I say a grateful...

Thank You.

Huldah's House, 2018

Butterfield Overland Mail route through the Murray farm.

Part of the lane which was the old Boonville Road and Butterfield Overland Mail Route.

www.ingramcontent.com/pod-product-compliance
Lightning Source LLC
Chambersburg PA
CBHW061739270326
41928CB00011B/2306